THE SCOUTING GUIDE TO TRACKING

THE SCOUTING GUIDE TO TRACKING

MORE THAN 100 ESSENTIAL SKILLS FOR IDENTIFYING AND TRAILING ANIMALS

BY LEN McDOUGALL

Skyhorse Publishing

Text and Photos Copyright © 2019 by Len McDougall
Logo Copyright © 2019 The Boy Scouts of America

Skyhorse Publishing books may be purchased in bulk at special discounts for sales promotion, corporate gifts, fund—raising, or educational purposes. Special editions can also be created to specifications. For details, contact the Special Sales Department, Skyhorse Publishing, 307 West 36th Street, 11th Floor, New York, NY 10018 or info@skyhorsepublishing.com.

Skyhorse® and Skyhorse Publishing® are registered trademarks of Skyhorse Publishing, Inc.®, a Delaware corporation.

Visit our website at www.skyhorsepublishing.com.

10 9 8 7 6 5 4 3 2 1

Library of Congress Cataloging-in-Publication Data is available on file.

Cover design by Brian Petersen

Print ISBN: 978-1-5107-3773-0
Ebook ISBN: 978-1-5107-3776-1

Printed in China.

TABLE OF CONTENTS

x

INTRODUCTION

Before learning the fun techniques described in this book, bear in mind that a tracker appreciates every aspect of nature, and abides by the Scouting motto of "Leave No Trace." Always respect wildlife and do not interfere with their natural habits. Everything that touches or moves over the earth leaves a sign of its passing (one old tracking proverb says that even an eagle can be tracked if it poops often enough). Since the earliest hominids (our ancestral humans) learned to live together in tribal communities, trackers were among a tribe's most highly regarded members. It was they who were relied upon to track the animals their brethren ate to within range of a primitive weapon, and then to continue to track them until they were rendered into meat.

Until the invention of modern hunting weapons, animals as large as deer did not often die with the first shot, especially if the weapon used was a bow and arrow or a lance. Even today, African Bushmen take it for granted that an antelope shot by their most skilled archer will need to be tracked for miles, and shot perhaps twice more before it dies. You can imagine how hard it was for Sioux hunters to take down a bison on the plains of western America.

The ability to track and read sign is the closest

Everything that moves over the earth, even under water, leaves a sign that it passed there; it falls to a tracker to recognize and follow those clues.

Still in use by aboriginal societies today, primitive bows are under-powered by modern archery standards, yet effective enough to keep entire tribes fed, providing hunters are also skilled trackers.

that any of us will come to having a genuine super power. That's why forensic crime scene investigation shows have been so popular on television. To come onto a scene and use only your own senses of sight, touch, smell, and even taste to interpret what happened before you got there can be a pretty impressive feat. A skilled tracker or forensics expert can not only tell what has happened, but how long ago it occurred, and sometimes a good deal more that escapes notice by an ordinary person. As TV ratings show, the ability to create a true story from evidence at or around a scene is pretty amazing to people who lack the expertise to do that themselves.

In the old West, a tracker could tell if the person being trailed was wearing a six gun, and even the hip on which he wore it. The gun itself didn't weigh enough to show in the tracks, but it made its wearer walk more heavily on that side, and to place that foot differently than the other. A similar occurrence happens if a person has a bow or camera bag slung over one shoulder; having the added bulk will make its wearer drag a foot slightly on that side.

Or a person may have a limp. A limp causes the foot on the side with the injury or deformity to hit the ground harder, leaving a deeper outer-heel imprint and usually with a more toes-inward track. However, a limp is an anomaly, and not all of them are identical, depending on their cause. A limp is identifiable, however, by being consistently abnormally different (anomalous) from a typical footstep.

Likewise if a person or an animal is injured on one leg, the prints left by that foot will be less heavily imprinted, usually twisted to one side as the bearer seeks to place the hurt foot so that it causes as little pain as possible. In most cases, the opposite, uninjured leg will bear more weight than usual, leaving extra-heavy foot impressions. All of this and more will be covered in detail in later chapters.

But tracking is far more than just interpreting footfall impressions in the earth. Everything that moves across or interacts in any way with the features of the land is bound to leave sign. A grouse may preen free one of its down feathers as it grooms itself on an overhead branch, or sometimes a sandhill crane or raven pulls free a flight feather as it probes its plumage for fleas.

A wolf, coyote, fox, or deer all shed their dense winter coats in clumps after each winter (March or April, depending on latitude, or how cold their normal climate is). These clumps of fur often get snagged by brush, or just fall free, as the animal passes through, especially if branches don't have leaves on them yet. This is where reading sign shows its value: tufts of wolf and coyote fur might be difficult to tell apart, especially since the two species have been interbreeding to create "coy-wolves" for nearly two decades. But a full-grown wolf stands a foot taller at the shoulder than a large coyote, so if the fur snagged is four feet above the ground, it's too high to have been left there by a shorter coyote.

Even a raven might leave a visible sign that it has been there when it pulls a feather free while preening itself on an overhead branch.

On the other hand, there have for centuries been beaver-toppled trees whose cut height is four or five feet above the ground, leading to stories of gigantic beavers. A tracker knows that those beavers were

normal size, they were just standing on top of two or three feet of hard-packed snow when they gnawed the tree down, making them seem that much taller when the snow is gone.

Or consider the rough black scars on the normally smooth-barked aspen trees in the western United States or the very similar poplar trees of the East. While white-tailed and mule deer winter primarily on cedar and pine foliage, elk (wapiti) and moose make a diet of tender smooth bark during the snowy months. Scarred, rough black patches of bark, often showing sidewise scrape marks from the grazing animals' bottom teeth (deer and bison lack top teeth), are a sure sign of elk or moose living in the area.

Squirrel hunters learned a long time ago, when any accurate rifle-bored muzzle-loading long arm of 45 caliber or less was commonly known as a "squirrel gun," and bushy-tailed tree-dwelling rodents often meant the difference between eating well and malnutrition, to take note of oak and other nut-bearing twigs that had been snipped free of their parent branches. Especially common in early to late autumn, when squirrels gather nutty, storable maple samaras ("whirligigs"), fruits from gnawed-open walnuts, hickory, and pecan nuts, twig ends, nipped off by the rodents' sharp, stepped incisors litter the ground beneath their parent trees. Savvy squirrel hunters have long known to just take a seat and wait for the animals to come down to retrieve their prizes.

Tufts of fur from an animal that's shedding its warm winter coat in preparation for summer often get snagged by branches as it passes through.

As this birch stump demonstrates, its trunk was gnawed through by beavers when there were different levels of snow on the ground.

Orchard owners wrap young, smooth-barked fruit trees with protective plastic to keep rabbits and hares from gnawing off the bark near ground level, especially in winter, and these species do the same to smooth-barked shrubs and trees in the wild.

Other obvious, but sometimes unrecognized signs include deer beds made from packed-down grasses, de-barked pieces of green branches left by beavers, fuzzy round beds on the ground where a litter of precocious (fast-growing) hares were recently born, and furry balls wrapped around small bones under a tree branch that were regurgitated by owls. If it sounds like there are enough animal tracks and signs to spend your entire life just learning them all, there are indeed.

But that's the beauty and the fascination of being a tracker. Some folks spend their entire lives watching and cataloging birds (ornithologists). Some, as previously mentioned, attend universities to learn similar skills for solving crimes as forensics investigators. Some collect coins (numismatists), some collect stamps (philatelists).

Being a plain old tracker is the coolest activity of them all, whether you're lucky enough and skilled enough to do it at a professional level, or just as a hobby. Tracking and reading sign is the epitome of what a Scout should be.

A tracker is never unprepared for the environment, be it mosquito-infested tundra, hip-deep snow, or an unpredicted flash flood. Likewise, if it's a possibility, a Scout should be ready to meet it, and if a Scout isn't ready to meet it, he sure should be ready to cope with it. A tracker can help to find lost people, while never becoming a victim himself. A tracker needs more than just survival tools, but that equipment will be covered later.

Not everyone lives in an environment that enables them to track bears or wolves. There is no education better than years of field experience, but the problem with that is that it takes years of field experience to get that education. This book offers a shortcut by packing a lifetime of tracking experience in one place, condensing years of useful information into a few pages that you can memorize, or at least reference as you need to.

A few generations ago, it was a Scout who rescued lost hikers, not the other way around; a tracker is by definition comfortable in any wilderness.

There was a time when the Scouts, even whole troops, were sometimes called upon to find victims who were lost in the wilderness and to assist in rescues after a flood or some other catastrophe. A Scout who can track, read sign, and make sense from his surroundings may provide valuable services to others in any number of situations. The contents of this book are intended to help Scouts and anyone else to become assistants to first responders, emergency services, and even the heroes that they can be.

In the meanwhile, learning to track and read sign is just plain fun, so take this book into the woods, to a city park, or even into your own backyard, and just have a good time.

USING THIS BOOK

To track down a wild animal on its own turf, using your own intelligence and skills to defeat an animal's superior senses, is one of the greatest thrills you can have. This field guide is intended to be a complete field reference for would-be trackers, who may need every technique and trick they can use to find, trail, and outwit the animals they track. Based on the theory that one picture can equal a thousand words, this book is heavily illustrated. Both photos and illustrations are used because drawings can sometimes better accentuate

Even a good photo is only two-dimensional, without depth, often unable to show important details that are visible to the eye. In such instances, a drawing might better illustrate the more important points.

important details, while a camera reproduces only two dimensions, without depth or distance. Where needed, illustrations have been used to highlight nuances, like differences in pressure and depth, that would be obvious in the field, but not in a photo.

The book is divided into two sections: First is a catalog of common characteristics and information that applies to nearly all animals, even on other continents (if you can recognize a cat track in North America, you'll at least know that a leopard track in Africa was made by a cat). Section Two contains specific data about game species in North America, including details that distinguish a species from other members of its taxonomic Family. Each section contains real-world tracking information arranged in a format that makes looking up answers in the field fast and easy.

Finally, this book is written in appreciation of Scouts, whose contribution and hard work have historically helped to preserve, restore, and foster an appreciation of natural treasures that everyone can enjoy. Not every tracker is a Scout, but every Scout and outdoorsman needs a working knowledge of tracking techniques.

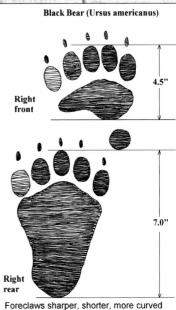

Black Bear (Ursus americanus)

Right front

4.5"

Right rear

7.0"

Foreclaws sharper, shorter, more curved than brown bear, enabling black bear to climb trees.

SECTION ONE

PRINCIPLES OF TRACKING AND READING SIGN

GENERICS OF ANIMAL TRACKS AND PHYSIOLOGY

Following creatures that move over land by the disturbances they leave is not an art, but a science comprised of empirical (known) information and quantifiable (measurable) data. Reading sign, which includes following footprints, is the original forensic science, where an investigator collects visual and other clues from the environment, then interprets and assembles those bits of knowledge, like a jigsaw puzzle, to form a picture of what happened there.

Most fundamental is learning to recognize sign when you see it. There has never been a tracker who hasn't been confounded when they showed someone else a track, only to have that person say "Where?" The illustrations and photos on these pages will help you to recognize partial tracks and disturbances.

The best trackers possess intimate knowledge of their prey's needs and habits. A moose tracker needs to know that the species will never be far from aquatic plants that are a mainstay of its diet, and a pronghorn hunter wouldn't bother looking for this open-range species in the deep woods. No species lives in a habitat that doesn't provide for its needs, and the better a place suits an animal's living requirements, the more likely that it will be found there.

Can you see the front and hind bear tracks in this photo? Many people whom you might show them to cannot, a constant source of frustration for a tracker. The more skilled you become, the more common this problem will be.

Generics of Animal Tracking

Nature is the very definition of order and logic; millions of years of natural selection ensure that nothing in it is without purpose, and trackers should always operate from a mindset that every mystery has a logical explanation. The advantage for a tracker is that successful adaptations tend to be repeated, regardless of species, and some are virtually universal, whether the animal is a fox or an elephant.

Front and hind tracks are usually easy to differentiate, because forefeet are noticeably larger in most species, particularly the fast runners. Reasons include a barrel chest that permits maximum lung volume while in flight or pursuit, but makes its owner front-heavy. Forefeet, which hit the ground first at a running gait, require greater surface area for traction and weight distribution (flotation) on snow and soft surfaces. Independently movable toes are generically tipped with hard keratin, usually in the form of claws or hooves, which serve as tools, weapons, brakes, and traction control when making abrupt changes in direction.

The Quadrupedal Design

Higher animals have four legs, never three or five, because countless generations have proved that the quadrupedal design is most effective for life on uneven ground. The design ensures that at least two feet are on the ground at all times, minimizing the chance of injuries, and maximizing balance. Quadrupeds typically have heavily muscled hind quarters that can propel them up to several times their own body lengths, resulting in running speeds—actually a series of leaps—that can surpass the fastest human by two or three times. Increased weight distribution also means greater stealth, because feet contact the ground more softly.

Paw Anatomy

A universal among pawed animals is segmented feet that have a heel pad, with no fewer than four, no more than five, toes. This arrangement has proved to be the ideal number for soft-pawed predators and prey that make a living running, climbing, and digging in rugged terrain. Toes can be splayed,

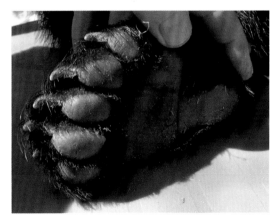

Brown Bear (Ursus arctos horribilis)

5.0"+ Front

10.0"+ Hind

Note similarity to Black Bear tracks.

In contrast, this drawing of brown bear tracks highlights points where a bear applies most of its weight, making it easier to decipher what you might be seeing in an otherwise confusing impression.

As this black bear cub's right hind foot clearly exemplifies, every animal is born having the tools and weapons with which to cope with its home environment.

spread wide to increase surface area on soft ground, or dug downward to maximize traction. The number of toes in a track is a valuable identifier. Carnivores designed for fast pursuit—the canids and the felids—travel on four toes. Omnivores that normally move with a shuffling gait, like weasels, bears, opossums, and raccoons, have five toes on all four feet. Squirrels (including marmots), rabbits, and hares have four toes on the forefeet, five on the hind feet. No normal pawed mammal has fewer than four toes or more than five.

This cougar's tracks show where it jumped down from a height, landing with most of its weight on its powerful front shoulders.

Hoof Anatomy

Hoofed animals, called ungulates, nearly always have two spreadable toes that can be splayed to form a braking wedge on slippery ground. The Equidae (horse) family, with its single toe, is a notable exception. Hooved animals fall into the orders Artiodactyla, those with an even number of toes, and Perrissodactyla, those with an odd number of toes. All deer, bovids, antelope, goats, and swine are cloven-hooved, with two forward-pointing toes, with or without (depending on the species) a pair of "dewclaws" at the rear of the ankles. Ungulates tend to be swift runners with an herbivorous diet (swine are omnivorous), all are sure-footed on frozen terrain, and most species tend to be social, traveling in groups. Despite the sometimes impressive stature of males in the deer family (Cervidae), the dominant animal in every herd will always be an adult female.

Weight Displacement

Four-legged animals walk with body weight concentrated on the outer edges of their soles, which maximizes the distance between contact points (straddle), and provides greater stability. This configuration, which is opposite the human design, means the outermost toe or hoof is larger and prints more heavily than the smallest innermost toe. Knowing this gives a tracker the means to distinguish between left and right prints. If a bear or wolf's largest toe is on the right in a track, the print was made by a right foot.

Digitigrade

A colloquialism for alertness is to "be on your toes," and its origins are rooted in the way animals designed to run fast tend to walk "digitigrade" fashion, with body weight habitually leaned forward to minimize the time required to go from motionless to top speed. The result is a track that registers more deeply at the toes than at the heels, and trackers should remember that on firmer ground only the toes may print. On firm ground, a moose track that registers only partially may be mistaken for a whitetail track. Species that are digitigrade include deer, canids (dogs), felids (cats), and generally any fast-running species.

Plantigrade

If you're not on your toes, you might be "caught flat-footed." Species that walk flat-footed are called "plantigrade," and are characterized by elongated hind feet that are not built for running speed or agility. Inefficient predators, most are omnivorous opportunists, with a defensive capability that makes fleeing from predators unnecessary; skunks have a chemical repellent, bears have brute power, porcupines have quills, and Homo sapiens mastered fire and weapons.

Track Patterns

The way all four footprints are arranged—the "track pattern"—tells how fast an animal was traveling. Differences in the track patterns of walking, trotting, and running animals reveal if an animal was relaxed, had a purpose, or was in flight (or injured). Track patterns for different gaits (speeds) are largely universal among four-legged mammals, with track placement for a coyote being similar to that of a whitetail in every gait.

How Quadrupeds Walk

Quadrupeds share similarities in the way they walk, trot, and run. To prevent foot injuries while walking, forefeet can be visually placed to avoid stepping into hazards. Hind feet, which cannot be easily seen, are then brought forward in the same line to land as closely as possible to the same safe spot just vacated by the forefoot on that side. At a walk, the forefoot and hind foot on opposite sides are brought forward at about the same time, planted securely, and used as pivot points while the opposite front and hind legs swing ahead for the next step. Pace lengths, known as "stride," can vary by several inches on uneven terrain. Be aware that different tracking authors measure stride differently, but in this book stride will be measured as the open, untracked space between the rear track's toes and the front track's heel.

"Straddle," the distance between left and right forefeet on a trail, is used to estimate an animal's chest width, but trackers need to know that deer, especially, establish and

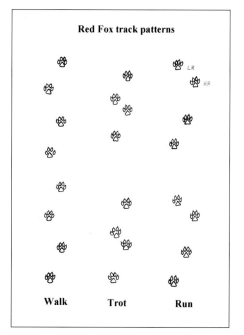

Red Fox track patterns

Walk   Trot   Run

A lot is revealed by the way a quadruped places its feet; not just how fast it's traveling, but its disposition (frightened, relaxed, hurried), and perhaps where it's heading.

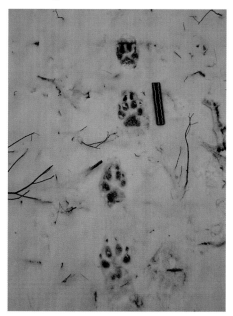

A wolf walking at a casual, relaxed pace.

travel on trails that are half the width of their makers. Walking, and trotting, with paws or hooves spread over as narrow an area as possible minimizes chance of injury on rough terrain by keeping the strength of both legs close together. It also enables quadrupeds to quickly create trails that permit fast, quiet travel, with minimal scent and sign. Of most importance to the tracker is knowing that an eight-hundred-pound elk can travel almost silently on the trails used by smaller whitetail or mule deer.

At a casual walk on flat ground, hind feet tend to register on top of foreprints, leaving both tracks in the same impression. Often, a hind foot registers slightly ahead of or behind a front track, leaving an elongated impression that trackers should be careful not to mistake as a single footprint. In most cases, the hind prints will be discernible because they overlay foreprints. Sometimes double-track impressions can be mistaken for single, very long footprints; a closer look at the species' track description and dimensions (Section Two) can prevent that problem.

How Quadrupeds Trot

At a trot, both hind feet and one forefoot typically print together in a loosely triangular configuration, with the remaining forefoot printing separately ahead of the others. This ensures that three feet hit the ground almost simultaneously, giving the stability of a tripod, while the remaining forefoot acts as a pivot when those three are brought forward. Which forefoot prints alone is an indication of whether the animal is right- or left-side dominant, which may help to identify individuals.

How Quadrupeds Run

At a full-out run, most quadrupeds adopt a "rocking horse" track pattern in which forefeet are planted closely together and act as a pivot when the rear feet are brought forward to land on either side of them. When the widely-stanced hind feet make contact, the animal lunges forward, forefeet together and stretched ahead to catch it after a leap that may exceed four times its body length. A unique exception is the mule deer's "rubberball" gait, in which all four feet are kept close together under the body, where they act as springs to propel the animal in a series of controlled bounces, each of which can exceed ten feet.

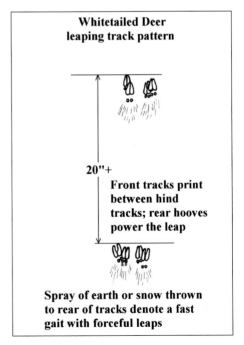

Whitetailed Deer leaping track pattern

20"+

Front tracks print between hind tracks; rear hooves power the leap

Spray of earth or snow thrown to rear of tracks denote a fast gait with forceful leaps

A typical white-tailed deer leaping track pattern.

Terrain Variations

Mud:

Wet mud, especially clay, is the best medium in which to find a clear track, because mud molds itself to the contours of an object pressed into it. This leaves a three-dimensional imprint that can be used to determine not only the size of the animal, but its approximate weight, details as faint as a scar or a limp, a broken claw or chipped hoof, and the definition to discern front and rear tracks in the same impression.

Snow:

Snow is a preferred tracking medium, because it covers everything, and animals walking on it usually leave a clear track. But there are different types of snow, and tracks can register much differently in them. The reason Eskimos have more than fifty words for snow is because snow can have that many states, from soft and packed, to hard and icy. One tip to remember is that the longer any animal stands motionless on snow, the deeper and sharper the track, and it often helps to know if and where that animal stood to observe its surroundings.

Fresh wet snow in temperatures near the freezing mark usually leaves a clear track, especially if the ground below is unfrozen, and shows at the bottom of prints. Good for making snowballs, this snow often registers a near perfect print. Be aware that warm snow tends to "grow" a track; depending on outside influences like rain, sun, warm air, and time of exposure, a track might grow to half again its actual size. This phenomenon is responsible for stories about giant deer or coyotes, and so on.

Powder snow in temperatures below 20°F is dust-like, and impressions may be as formless as tracks in dry sand. Stride and straddle measurements can help to identify species and size, but clearer tracks are usually found by following the trail to a place where snow is less deep, and impressions are less filled in by loosened snow.

Late-winter "hardpack" snow that has compressed under its own weight may also fail to register a readable track, especially between sunset and dawn, when nighttime cold can give snow the hardness of concrete. On this medium it may be necessary to inspect prints from very close up, looking for claw marks, hoof edges, and other disturbances that can be assembled into a complete picture.

Deep snow results in a series of holes, with tracks hidden at the bottom. Stride lengths are not representative when each step is a struggle, and gait usually consists of a series of leaps, because it is easier to jump upward and ahead than to push legs through such resistance. "Depth of trough," the impression made by an animal's chest, is sometimes used to guess at its size, but the best strategy is to follow a trail to firmer ground, where footprints show clearly. No animal prefers to plow through deep snow, and those that do are almost certainly headed to a place with more solid footing.

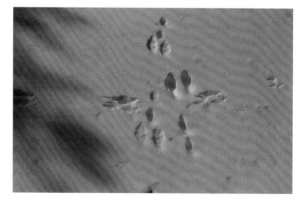

Snow can either be a perfect tracking medium, or it can be an impossible surface to track over; there's a reason that Eskimo tribes have so many words for "snow."

Sand:

Like snow, sand can register either a perfect impression or an unidentifiable track. In dry beach sand, an animal's tracks may be little more than small craters, while wet sand can yield a perfect track. Measuring stride and straddle between craters helps to identify their maker. Whenever possible a tracker should try to follow a trail until he can find an identifiable impression in soil that holds a track's details. Stream banks and lake shores are good places to find prints that are defined well enough to show scarred toes, chipped hooves, or broken claws that can even identify individual animals.

Forest humus:

As many Border Patrol officers learned when their presence was increased along the US-Canadian border after 9/11, deep forest is a tough place to track. The dead leaves and vegetation that comprises forest humus seldom registers more than a faint portion of any track, and what impressions are there will soon disappear.

Hooved animals (and booted human feet) leave the most obvious prints, but even these are likely to be little more than sharp-sided indentations in dead leaves. The sharper a hoof print's features, the fresher it is. Vegetation crushed underfoot helps to age a track: Fresh, wet plant tissue says the track is within a few hours old; browning, recently-green leaves and yellowed grass stems age the track at more than a day; brown, flattened dead plants have been walked on numerous times, and a trail is probably visible.

Bracken ferns (Pteridium aquilinum) are one of the most widespread vascular, or veined, plants in North America from spring to autumn, even further, and all year long in places that get only a few inches of snow in winter. The plants' green umbrella foliage can grow up to two feet above the ground on any wooded land, sometimes thick enough to completely hide the ground below. Bracken ferns are a tracker's friend because their long, fibrous stems are brittle (never pull up ferns with un-gloved hands; these fibers can cut skin like a razor). Any human or animal bigger than a raccoon cannot pass through them without breaking at least some of the ferns' stems, not only revealing its

Ferns are common, and they are a tracker's friend; this fern was broken more than a day ago by a deer traveling to the left in this photo.

passage but in which direction it was traveling, because the broken stems will point in that direction. Length of time since the stems were broken can also be determined: If a stem is wet at the break, passage was recent, within the last two to three hours. If the break is green and dry, it's about six hours old. If a break is yellowed, with fibers showing, it was broken eight to ten hours ago. If a break is turning black, it's about twelve hours old. If it's brown and dead, broken free easily, the fern was knocked over a day ago or more.

Pawed animals typically leave only faint, slightly flattened marks on leaves and humus as they walk over it, but often their claws will visibly displace leaves and debris. A twig or stone displaced from where it has laid long enough to make a depression indicates that it was kicked or rolled underfoot.

Dry leaves that have slid away to reveal moist or differently colored leaves beneath tell of an animal walking in the direction opposite the slide, and perforations made by non-retractable claws can be seen as evenly arrayed punctures in dead leaves (cats do not normally leave claw marks).

A track in mud or wet sand is often perfect, showing even the most minute details of its maker's foot.

Swamp is actually easier to track than hardwood forest, even though the country is more overgrown, because so much of it can register tracks. Carpets of sphagnum moss can hold an identifiable impression for about a day, and soft, wet soil will keep clear tracks until they are erased by more tracks or washed away.

Casting Tracks

At some point every tracker will want to take a track back home for further study, and that means "casting." This means pouring the plaster in a semi-liquid state that will flow into a track impression's recesses, then waiting for it to harden into a negative copy of the print. The result is a more or less accurate (depending on how clear the track) replica of the maker's foot.

Most tracks are cast from plaster of Paris. This powder is an inexpensive commodity in most arts-and-crafts and hardware stores. The slightly coarser, and more durable patching plaster (Durabond) used by drywallers is available at home improvement stores. One pound of either carried in a zippered bag inside a snap-top plastic container will cast a half-dozen or more tracks. The plastic bag helps to keep the plaster powder dry, while the plastic dish serves as a mixing bowl.

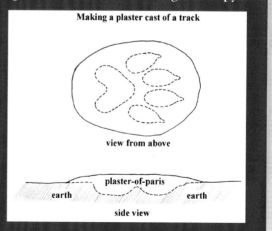

At some point everyone who gets bitten by the tracking bug will want to make a plaster cast of a track.

Casting a track in plaster isn't complicated: Dump about four tablespoons of plaster from the plastic bag into the mixing dish, and add water a little at a time, always blending it well into the plaster before adding more, until the mixture has the consistency of cake batter. Some trackers carry stir sticks for mixing plaster, but most environments will provide one. When the plaster is ready, dump it into a track impression and wait until it sets up; this will take roughly half an hour, longer in wet conditions, less in very cold temperatures that freeze the plaster before it actually hardens. Don't press the wet plaster into the track depression or you might deform the track's features; if your "batter" is the right consistency, it will flow into nooks and crannies on its own.

When the plaster has set, gently loosen it by cutting the soil or snow around it with a knife blade (never go into the woods without a working-class knife). Don't try to pry the cast loose, but rather lift it free by cutting around it, taking the entire track itself if necessary. Later, when the plaster is fully cured after a day or so, the cast will be a bit less fragile, but many a cast has been ruined before it ever got out of the woods. Place the cast, earth, or snow and all, into a plastic dish lined with folded paper towels (or reusable cloths) that act as cushions, place another cushion on top, and snap the lid in place.

In a few cases, like hard-frozen mud or slushy snow that has since frozen to ice, it may be impossible to cut around a cast in the ground, and you'll be forced to lift it from the impression. For this delicate operation you'll need to first use a "mold release," typically an aerosol can of wax that creates a soft, slippery film between impression and plaster. Wax sprays made for this purpose have not always performed well, sometimes spitting blobs of wax that can leave indentations in the cast that are not in the track, and the problem worsens in freezing temperatures. Better and cheaper in freezing temperatures are furniture wax sprays. In either instance, aerosol cans should be kept warm, carried inside the jacket if necessary.

Functions of a Tail

For most species, a tail is a valuable asset. In all cases, it covers the vulnerable anal and genital region, sometimes (as with coyotes) even wrapping between the legs to help protect the belly. For cougars and fishers, a long tail helps to maintain balance when the footing is narrow. The opossum's tail is prehensile, able to wrap around and grasp objects. The cervids (deer) have tails that are dark topside, in the down position, but starkly white below to serve as a visual beacon for herd members, especially offspring, to follow when danger threatens. Gray wolves keep their long tails straight back when hunting, so as not to alert prey, but raise or tuck it as required for social interaction with pack members (wolves never curl their tails over their backs, the way dogs can). Otters, beavers, and muskrats use their tails as rudders so that they might better concentrate their strength on swimming.

Tails can also help a tracker. Low-slung species, like raccoons, beavers, and porcupines, often drag their tails when walking; the whisk-broom brushing of a porcupine's tail is obvious on sand, but all long-tailed species have a tendency to sweep against the environment, sometimes leaving drag marks, hairs, and other disturbances.

Natural Tools and Weapons

Wild animals are born with the tools needed to render an environment into forms that suit their needs for survival and procreation. All have claws, teeth, beaks, or other natural tools that dig, grip, tear, or kill to get the things their owner needs to live, and the marks left by those natural tools may reveal the species, gender, age, and even the individual.

Claws are nature's original multi-function tools, and their structure helps to reveal a species' lifestyle. A black bear's sharply hooked claws allow it to snag smaller fish more efficiently than a grizzly, while stout construction allows them to rip apart rotting trees to find edible insects, or to clamber up tree trunks to raid honeybee nests or to escape enemies. The powerful, almost straight claws of a grizzly tell of a diet that requires digging to unearth edible roots, ground squirrels, and marmots, its main sources of meat when fish are not spawning.

This log, ripped apart by a black bear searching for edible insects, demonstrates that bears are well equipped to work within their environment.

Hooves are not predatory weapons, but animals that have them know instinctively to use them as bludgeons against adversaries. Trackers may also note that hooves are digging tools: Hogs use them to unearth edible roots; wintering deer use theirs to kick through crusted snow to reach grasses and break ice from watering holes; many species use their hooves to plow up the soil of scent posts.

Canines always mark a meat-eater, even though some powerful species that possess canines, like bears and pigs, are considered omnivorous, able to eat plants and almost anything organic. These mating pairs of pointed corner teeth serve to grasp prey, to deliver crushing puncture wounds, and as tools for ripping hide and flesh. Behind them are "carnassial" teeth, or very sharp premolars, whose scissor-like action can cut tough hide, and are invaluable for severing the joint ligaments and tendons of prey. Heavier molars at the jaw's rear can crush bones to obtain rich marrow, leaving gouges in a bone's surface.

Herbivores typically have chisel-like incisors that are designed to remove bites of vegetation. In rodents and lagomorphs (e.g., rabbits and hares), these consist of "buck" teeth in which two pairs of large overlapping incisors (front teeth) on top and bottom work to efficiently snip through twigs, bark, and tough stems. Biting through twigs makes a distinctive stepped cut; scraping edible bark from shrubs leaves twin gouges. Note, too, that many chisel-tooth species, especially porcupines and red squirrels, gnaw shed antlers and larger bones to obtain nutrients that are lacking in their normal diet.

Deer and bovines (cattle, bison, water buffalo) do not have upper incisors. Instead, they have lower incisors that pin clumps of grasses against a hard upper palate, tearing them free and leaving ragged blades that are easy to identify. This arrangement is also well-suited to stripping leaves and evergreen foliage from branches, usually leaving scrape marks in the underside.

Reading Tracks

Deciphering paw and hoof impressions is fundamental to tracking, and a single print can yield considerable information, although it is never good strategy to rely on a single hoof, paw, or foot print to provide enough information. Always follow a trail at least several yards before making decisions about an animal's gender, size, age, intent, and so on.

Most species have a foot shape that is unique, different even from related species of the same family. The two-lobed heel pad of a gray wolf leaves a markedly different impression than the three-lobed heel pad of a coyote, differences in size notwithstanding (wolf tracks are very much larger than coyote tracks). Moose tracks have a split-hape shape, very similar to the much smaller whitetail and mule deer, but different than the concave hooves of an elk, whose tracks print most deeply at the outer edges, forming an almost split-circle shape. Furthermore, the split-circle elk print is more pronounced (rounder) in eastern low-woodland elk than it is in western mountain dwellers.

The first step is to "cut sign," that is, to find a trail left by the animal you want to find. In some environments, like tall grass and shrubby undergrowth, clear tracks might be invisible from just a few feet, but there must be a "trough" that was made when an animal's bulk pushed aside vegetation during its passage. The trick is to "look wide," never focusing your eyes in one place, but taking in everything, allowing your advanced human vision system to automatically detect anomalies in terrain. Grasses that lean the wrong way, dead twig ends that are snapped off, sticks that are broken in a downward direction, flower petals on the ground, anything that indicates recent disturbance. With a little experience, you'll be able to spot and follow many game trails without seeing a single track.

Even solid rock registers sign, not in the form of prints, but as disturbances created by an animal's feet. Left untouched for a few days, sometimes just a few hours, rock becomes dusted with fine airborne granules of sand that are displaced by the slightest contact. Both paws and hooves reveal themselves as scrape marks, with most sand pushed rearward, opposite the direction of travel. Displaced stones and sticks that have laid long enough for their top sides to be bleached by sun will be obvious by their darker undersides, as will the contrasting spots where they had been.

Cutting sign can also be done on paved roads, even from a slow-moving vehicle. Early morning, when most species move from feeding to sleeping places, is especially productive, because animals with dew-wet feet will pick up a covering of sand from the shoulder. As they walk across the harder asphalt, sand will fall away, leaving negative outlines that may be very accurate representations of the animal that made them.

If you know the dimensions of an average track for the species being sought, track size can be an indicator of age, probable gender (male mammals tend to be larger than females), and an animal's age up to adulthood. Except for size differences, gender cannot be determined from a track, but will likely be made evident by other behaviors along the trail—another reason that you need to follow a trail at least several yards before concluding anything. At breeding time, males of every polygamous species run constantly in pursuit of mates, and their exhaustion manifests itself as scuffed prints and toes that drag the ground when stepping forward.

THE ROLE OF SCENTS

Scents are a major part of every wild animal's language. Males and females alike employ urine, which has a fingerprint-like uniqueness in every individual, to broadcast territorial claims, advertise readiness to mate, and to bond with others in a social group.

Mammals, as well as reptiles and amphibians, and even birds, possess musk-producing glands located at strategic points on their bodies to signal hormonal changes and moods—particularly fear. Scent glands are commonly located at the cheeks (preorbital glands), at the base of the tail (precaudal, supracaudal, or violet gland), inside each rear knee (tarsal glands), and in the genital area (perianal or perineal glands). Interdigital (literally, "between the toes") glands on the soles produce an identification scent, but also leave behind a lasting smell of fear should their owner be frightened into flight, much like the sweaty palms experienced by a person who is scared. This serves to warn others in its herd or pack of danger in the area.

The world of smells that most animals live by is a difficult dimension for scientists to study, because it's so far beyond our sensory frame of reference as to seem supernatural. The olfactory powers common to wild creatures enables them to detect objects and animals that are hidden from their eyes, sometimes to distances beyond ten miles. More experienced animals can be expected to have the best education about what a scent belongs to, and increased ability to zero-in on its source.

While we are denied access to the olfactory world of wildlife, research and observation have yielded considerable information about the roles scents play in communication with wild species across the board. Some, like territorial and mating scents, may be strong enough to be detected by a human nose at several yards, while others may be identifiable by accompanying sign, like the mud and grass scent mounds of male beavers, or the housecat-like scratching and pungent urine spray of a cougar against a tree trunk. Like animals, humans can compile a catalog of recognizable odors through experience, but we can also learn to recognize and interpret the physical sign that frequently accompanies scent messages.

Territorial Scents

Territorial scents, mostly in the form of urine-borne hormones or glandular secretions from the anal region, are often undetectable by the human nose from even a few feet. Unlike sexual scents whose purpose is to bring in prospective mates from afar, territorial scents serve essentially as a fence that warns potential competitors not to cross this line.

Cats are the easiest to track down by their potent musky odors, and bears in the area can often be detected the same way during their mid-summer mating season. But determining if a male coyote recently cocked its leg against a tree in summer may require pressing one's nose close to the base of a suspect tree and sniffing. Likewise, smelling for urine on or around a whitetailed deer's bed can reveal the animal's sex because does tend to step to one side to urinate upon rising, while bucks usually urinate directly onto the bed.

This adult gray wolf is a Beta (having a social status within the pack hierarchy); this wolf is scenting itself with the urine odor of an Alpha (pack leader) in the hope of making itself smell more important.

Male canids (coyotes, wolves, foxes, dogs) especially tend to urinate as high up on a tree as they can in an effort to make themselves appear as tall as possible to potential rivals. Whitetailed bucks carry information about their size, sexual disposition, and perhaps more, in their urine, and it's probable that other species do the same.

Mating Scents

Odors emitted by an animal for the purpose of attracting a mate are frequently strong enough for a person to smell from several yards or more because their intent is to broadcast the sexual availability of their maker over as wide an area as possible. Nearly all sexual scents share a strong musky characteristic that has been described as skunklike by some, and like the smell of housecat urine by others. Either way, mating scent posts are often fragrant enough to permit finding them by scent alone.

Males of most species complement their sexual scent posts with a visual advertisement comprised of materials from the surrounding environment. Bull elk wallow in urine- and feces-scented mud; bull moose (and elk) adorn their antlers with uprooted vegetation. Boar bears claw as high as they can reach on tree trunks. Male (and dominant, or Alpha, female) wolves and coyotes scratch their paws against the earth after urinating.

Danger Scents

Not much is known about the proverbial smell of fear except that it is indeed a reality in the animal world. What little hard information that exists has been established mostly about whitetailed deer, because retail sales of hunting aids to whitetail hunters has become an industry profitable enough to fund the research and development of new products.

It is known that interdigital glands located between a deer's cloven hooves exude a hormone that fellow deer recognize as fright. This gives other whitetails a heads-up that danger was recently there, causing smarter individuals among them to avoid that area in case a predator might still be lying there in wait. The same kind of interdigital excretion can be seen in the sweaty palms and soles of feet of humans who are afraid or nervous.

Camouflage Scents

Probably every dog owner has seen a dog or cat rolling exuberantly on something we wish they hadn't touched. The powerful stench of rotting fish carcasses is preferred by all breeds, but sometimes scat or garbage also triggers the

This whitetailed fawn is not just fleeing, it's leaving a scent of fear behind through interdigital glands located between its hooves.

rolling behavior among wild canids and an occasional wild or domestic cat. This behavior, common to carnivorous mammals, helps to fool prey into believing that a hunter moving in for the kill is already dead, and therefore not a threat.

Some animals also scent themselves with aromatic plants. Bobcats roll in catnip beds, canids seem drawn to juniper, and many species purposely rub sticky pine sap onto their fur (pine sap also helps to repel ticks and fleas). Male deer in rut spar with pines, getting sap on their antlers. In places where leeks and onions grow, the plants themselves are odorous enough to defeat a keen sense of smell.

ANALYZING SCATS

Much can be learned from an animal's poop. Scat is matter that was eaten, but wasn't converted to usable nutrients by the digestive tract. This undigested material can tell trackers a lot about the individual animal from whence it came. Cougar and wolf scats are nearly identical in shape and size, wrapped in a spiral sheath of prey fur that cleans the intestines while protecting them from sharp objects encased safely within. Breaking either apart usually reveals small bones, because both species swallow mouse-size prey whole, but if the interior of the scat contains chunks of a deer's leg bone, the predator had powerful jaws built for crushing, which rules out a cougar. Note that wolves, dogs, and to a lesser extent, coyotes and foxes, can digest many raw bones

What comes out of an animal can tell an immense amount about that animal, like this black bear's rectal plug that keeps the maker from defecating inside its den during it long winter sleep; the bear's last meal before hibernation consisted of rodents before it ate the undigestible plug of dead swamp grasses.

(especially deer) that they are capable of crushing into small bits in their jaws, resulting in gray-colored scat.

Scat Location

While scats might seem to be randomly placed, closer examination shows that their locations are by natural design, and there is purpose to every pattern. With so much of every species' communications dependent on scent, scat, and its placement, scat plays a vital role in marking or laying claim to a place.

Predator scats are strategically placed at trail intersections as boundary markers to discourage competitors for that area's resources. Trackers who find predator scat on a hiking trail can expect to find an intersecting trail that crosses there. Boundary scats most often belong to males; females are naturally more exclusive, and tend not to claim a domain unless rearing young. These scat posts serve to visually warn potential competitors that this territory is claimed, and carry an olfactory biography of the maker's gender, age, and size, helping to minimize challenges to his dominance. Every summer, in front of our rural mailbox, there is a frequently refreshed black bear scat, a clear territorial boundary mark.

That olfactory calling card also helps to make males of some species stand out at mating time; during their October-November rut, bull elk employ scats as part of the bath of mud, urine, and scat that every contending male covers himself with to maximize chances of being noticed. For whitetails and hares, whose scats are left at random along a spider web of trails that become more numerous closer to feeding areas, the advantage is that everything smells like them. If a pursuing predator loses sight of its prey for even a second, it will probably not be able to reacquire it by scent in that maze of smells.

Interpreting Diet from Scats

Some of what goes into a creature inevitably comes out in identifiable form. Soft, black raccoon scat with a sprinkling of small whitish seeds say that the animal has been feeding in a nearby raspberry patch. In places that produce blueberries (July through September), expect that scats from even carnivores will be distinctly purple, often with undigested berries throughout.

Cowpie-like moose and elk scats say that the animals have been eating their fill of rich vegetation, especially apples, which upsets their digestive tracts and narrows the places a tracker would look to find those animals during feeding hours.

Porcupine scats that resemble pellets strung together like beads reveal that this nocturnal feeder has been grazing in open, grassy places, probably where blades are thickest and most succulent. Cat or canine scats encased in a spiral of fine fur, with very small leg and other bones, tell of a diet of rodents, while coarse fur with large fragments of crushed

Predator scats, like this red fox deposit, are never just left haphazardly, but are strategically left at territorial boundaries and at other important claims.

Some natural prey animals like whitetailed deer, rabbits, and hares do precisely the opposite of predators, depositing their scats everywhere they travel, leaving a confusing maze of scents to confound the noses of hunters.

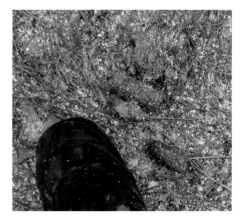

This unusual bear scat shows that its maker was feeding heavily on carrots from a deer hunter's bait pile.

leg bone inside say that this large carnivore was probably a bear or a wolf (maybe a wolverine in northern latitudes).

Remember that both cats and dogs eat some vegetation (blueberries are an almost universal favorite among birds and animals), and predators frequently eat grass. The coarse, indigestible cellulose fibers work to scrub clean the intestines, much like the "fiber" that is a popular part of human diets. Be cautious not to mistake grass fibers for animal fur.

Interpreting Health from Scats

Scats can be an indicator of an animal's health. A bear whose scat is dry and fibrous in autumn, maybe with a mucous coating, is not feeling well, probably not fat enough to survive the coming winter, and likely an old, arthritic individual that could be malnourished and potentially dangerous. Brown bear student Timothy Treadwell, of *Grizzly Man* fame, was almost certainly killed and eaten by such a bear back in 2003 in Katmai National Park, Alaska.

Predator scats, especially, may contain whitish parasitic worms, or segments of flatworms (usually tapeworms), which tells a hunter or trapper that this individual's compromised body is probably not in prime condition. A scat that is watery and loose denotes an irritated digestive system. It is never a good idea to handle scats with bare hands, and be especially cautious around scats that look unhealthy, because many parasites and diseases are transmittable to humans. Some, like a bloodborne fungus called Blastomycosis, is serious, and often fatal.

While loose scats don't necessarily indicate illness greater than an upset stomach, healthy scats are always formed and firm. Shape is always roughly cylindrical or rounded, reflecting the shape and diameter of the organs that produce it. An abundance of grasses, nature's own dietary fiber, in carnivore scats reveals a need to scrub undigested material from the animal's lower digestive tract, and are especially prevalent with older individuals.

Again, do not handle scats with your bare hands. Infectious organisms are common in scats, including intestinal flagellates like Giardia, intestinal cysts like

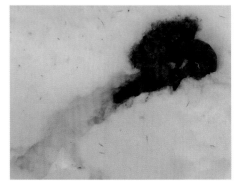
This scat came from an ailing animal, probably one with a perforated and bleeding intestine caused by eating a sharply pointed bone fragment.

The canine that made this scat also deposited numerous health-threatening whipworms, indicating its less than ideal state of health.

For health reasons, never handle scats with bare hands.

Cryptosporidium, even very dangerous brain worms. If you need to break apart a scat sample to examine its contents, wear disposable plastic or nitrile gloves, and use a stick to open the deposit.

Aging Scats

Scat color is dependent on food color. As noted, many species leave purple scats in blueberry country, but fresh carnivore scat that is black, with little or no fur, denotes a large prey animal and a meal of pure flesh, and fresh deposits will sometimes smell of rotting meat. Crushed bones show as chunks of white, or sometimes as a grayish area of mostly-digested powdered bone. Spherical rabbit pellets that are green tell that their maker was frightened off before it could re-ingest them for final digestion (a process known as caecal fermentation; yes, rabbits and hares re-eat their poop); completely digested scat pellets are dark brown.

Whatever color a scat is, it will lighten in color with exposure to air. Fast-decaying organics, like meat and skin, are the first to decompose, becoming paler as time passes, until those materials turn ash-white and crumble. Tougher hairs, grass, and plant fibers remain intact for up to several months, but also pale with age. How quickly a scat fades depends on environmental influences: In hot weather, the process can take only two days; colder weather can slow decay for up to several weeks, and scats left atop snow remain fresh-looking until spring thaw. In spring, recently thawed scats frequently grow moldy.

Fresh scats are generally dark in color, but will invariably become lighter in color as they age.

4

READING SIGN

Reading footprints is the most romanticized part of tracking, but visible clues to following a creature's route are not limited to paw or hoof impressions. Furbearers shed and grow seasonal coats in response to seasonal temperature changes, and, in spring especially, shed fur is often caught in tree bark. Small patches of moist leaves that contrast with a dry, lighter-colored top layer must have been made by an animal; a closer look could reveal a regular series of disturbances, which can then be for stride and straddle, and used to determine what, and even which, animal passed there. When trailing an animal afield, recognizing the visible impact it leaves on the environment can be invaluable.

This is not a track, but this ripped-apart log is a clear indication that a bear was recently here looking for edible insects.

Feeding Sign

The fed-upon carcass of an adult elk is a sure sign that large predators are nearby—probably close enough to resent the appearance of another predator (including yourself). Never approach the carcass of a large animal unless it has been stripped clean (use binoculars), and even then do so with the utmost caution.

None of the deer or bovine families in North America have upper incisors, only lower incisors with a hard upper palate that makes them tear off mouthfuls of grass and vegetation. Unlike rodents and rabbits, whose sharp upper and lower incisors snip off plants like scissors, grazing animals leave grasses and plants with fibrous, torn ends that are wet when fresh, becoming progressively drier, yellow, then brown or black as the plant heals and regenerates.

Carnivores, by definition, eat other animals, but all of them have some vegetation in their diets to provide nutrients not obtained from flesh, and most ingest rough grasses on occasion to help clean the digestive tract or induce vomiting. A yearly phenomenon in blueberry country is the way nearly every species' scats—even birds—turns purple from mid-summer to fall.

Think, too, of a species' physiology. Black and brown bears possess a long and convoluted digestive system that enables them to digest the roughest foods, but is susceptible to injury from sharp objects; one bear trademark is a squirrel or marmot carcass that has been entirely consumed except for claw-bearing feet. With less articulate paws, and a comparatively straight digestive tract, wolves, coyotes, and foxes can swallow small animals whole and ingest food in as large a portion as can be swallowed. Wolves enjoy the strength of a team, and large carcasses are often skinned by an anchor wolf with canines embedded through the nasal bones (rostrum), while another yanks the hide rearward.

Whether killed by a predator or a car, carcasses are fed on and stripped to bone by scavengers, and the sign left on even cleaned carcasses can tell a lot about what fed there. A coyote will scrape meat from bone and gnaw rib ends to get fat-rich marrow, but lacks the jaw power to crush larger bones for their marrow, the way a wolf or bear can. With cats, the bones may be wet and fresh, yet stripped clean of meat by a rasp-like tongue—as opposed to the tiny shreds of flesh that are left clinging to bone by pecking birds.

Carnivore researchers have found that predators seldom prefer to eat large kills in the same places where they were brought down or found, but drag or carry them into a secluded thicket. Coyotes can carry nothing larger than a hare, but gray wolves can lock onto the ribcage and spine of a seventy-five-pound whitetail carcass and carry it a quarter-mile before feeding.

Some feeding sign makes obvious changes to the environment; wild cherries are a favorite autumn food for bears, and trees bearing them will frequently be broken, even split down the middle, by the powerful animals as they bring the fruits within reach. Broken twigs and branches still on the tree were probably caused by a climbing raccoon as it reached for fruits. Clipped twig ends lying on the ground were nipped off by rodents (squirrels, porcupines, groundhogs), that then climbed down to retrieve the berries.

Mating Sign

Mating sign tends to be obvious for every species, because the goal is to attract as much attention as possible from the opposite sex. From the brightly colored head of a rutting tom turkey and the spreading-wing displays of a gander, to the scratching posts of a lynx, and the pungent odor of a wallowing bull elk, males are ostentatious. With few exceptions—like wolves and geese—males are typically polygamous, breeding with as many females as possible before seasonal hormones subside. Females typically maintain a much lower profile during mating season and feed even more heavily in preparation for pregnancy. That leaves males to pursue females, and some do that to exhaustion. The most dominant males are often too fatigued to step high, dragging their toes while stepping forward, kicking and marking low obstacles that would normally be cleared, and sometimes slipping on uneven terrain. Tired male deer may even leave a trail of kicked-up divots in grass or moss.

Some mating sign is also territorial, because territoriality and ritual combat help to insure that only the fittest animals will reproduce. Whitetail bucks are noted for making "scrapes" at the edges of their territories, patches of pawed up, usually damp, earth that are scented with hormone-laden urine. Male black bears in the summer rut mark territory by reaching as high as they can to claw standing trees (usually dead), leaving an interdigital scent from the paws and visual clues about the ruling male's size and strength.

Bedding Sign

Every animal must sleep, and most prefer a specific environment or location. By knowing the needs and normal habits of a species being sought, a tracker can station himself, or stalk into, places where his prey feels most relaxed, and is likely to move about during daylight hours. Because these safe places are usually in thickly overgrown terrain, there are only a few well-traveled trails through bedding places, and they will be used by every local inhabitant.

With few exceptions, mammals prefer to sleep in places that are concealed and shadowed, but afford a good view of the surrounding terrain. For squirrels, that will be a den or arboreal nest; bears and deer lay up in dense thickets, where superb olfactory senses and noisy forest debris help to ensure that no enemy gets within striking distance undetected.

A recently created oblong depression crushed down in tall sawgrasses tells that an animal slept there, its size and probable age, an estimate of its weight, and maybe even if it was a pregnant female. A deer-size bed of flattened leaves on a wooded hillside may have belonged to wolf lying in ambush, and it's probable that a wolf hunting large prey from ambush was not alone. If the bed belonged to a member of the deer family, bear in mind that males advertise themselves, especially during the rut, and, upon rising, a buck typically urinates onto his bed. Does and cows, who are often pregnant and vulnerable, tend to avoid scenting themselves except during the rut, and do not normally urinate on their own beds.

Environmental Disturbances

Animals sometimes get an itch, and furred species that grow heavy coats to guard against winter's chill are especially anxious to dislodge them in early summer. Warm sun causes dead winter fur to scratch against the skin, prompting the wearer to rub it free on rough-barked trees, rocks, even utility poles. Discarded fur can help to identify the species, and hairs caught in slivered wood or tree bark can give an estimate of height. Also valuable is knowing that old fur remains intact for several months, and, depending on migratory habits, the animal that shed it will be back that way again, maybe tonight. Be alert for good tracks at scratching posts, left when the animal shoved hard against the earth while moving its body.

Buck or bull rubs, made when antlered animals shred the bark of small trees while scraping off the dead "velvet" tissue that nurtures antlers through the summer, are a visible sign that male deer are around. All antlered species make an effort to clean their racks to polished bone before autumn's mating season, simultaneously scenting the saplings they scrape with hormonal scents from glands located on the forehead. Desiccated brown skin with a velvety texture on one side will usually be found at the site. Rubs can provide an estimate of the maker's size by how far scrape marks reach up a trunk, and there are always heavy tracks. Contending males may rub the same sapling, or another sapling close by, a challenge that helps to keep both males too preoccupied with each other to notice a tracker. Some branches show signs of abuse from being sparred with by antlers.

A typical buck rub, showing where bark has been scraped off of a sapling by a buck that used the tree to polish its antlers.

GENERIC ANIMAL BEHAVIORS

How Animals Behave

Thinking like his or her prey is key to any tracker's success, and the importance of knowing the details of that species' behavior cannot be overstressed. Fortunately many of the basics of life are generic, and these should be the first facts that a tracker commits to memory. Every animal needs water to live, so open water must be part of almost every species' habitat. Every animal needs food, and plant life is crucial, not only to the herbivores and omnivores that subsist on vegetation, but to the carnivores that hunt them. Adults of nearly every species claim an exclusive territory that contains enough food, water, and space to permit mating and rearing of young, and every territorial animal defends its domain against intruders that compete for its resources.

Life in the wild is tough, and the animals that live there tend to do things the easy way, conserving energy for times when it is needed. Left undisturbed, every species falls into routines that make daily activities the least strenuous. Game trails are called that because every established path is an often-used route by at least one, and probably many, species; if an animal walked it in one direction this morning, it will probably return in the opposite direction this evening. Established trails permit quiet, leisurely travel because debris that would make noise underfoot has already been snapped, crushed, or kicked aside, and they allow fast runners to flee or pursue at top speed through tangled jungle.

Left undisturbed, animals of all species fall into routines, just like people, establishing trails and habits that are convenient to them and predictable to a tracker who scouts them.

Territorial Behaviors

With rare exceptions (like armadillos), every animal must be territorial, because laying exclusive claim to an area serves numerous important functions in the animal world: Most obvious is possession of sufficient food and water, and a secure space in which to survive, mate, and raise offspring. But the territorial instinct also serves to prohibit inbreeding that might weaken a species' gene pool, and helps to insure that only the strongest adults are permitted to procreate.

To prevent trespassers, territories must be marked, especially at their edges, and to be most effective, those markings must be obvious. Because the most long-range sense for most species is smell, territorial markings are usually odorous, even to a human nose, and often visible. With both of those characteristics, scats are the most used markers; predators leave scats at trail intersections, and a tracker who finds predator scat on a hiking path should be alert for the animal trail that crosses it.

Most territories are claimed by males, or by females with young. Species of the deer family are one exception in which the dominant animal will always be a doe or cow, with authority over the largest males. Competitors for a territory's resources are always met with a threat of violence; female deer, especially, tend to resolve disputes with kicking matches that can be brutal. Males of every species tend to be less violent; intruders are challenged, but most arguments are settled through posturing and body language, because a real fight between two closely matched adversaries could result in both animals seriously injured.

A black bear's claw marks on this poplar tree are another territorial claim, placed as high up on the tree's trunk as the animal can reach to advertise its size to possible competitors.

Feeding Behaviors

Food is the most constant need in every animal's daily life, and one commodity that every species will be possessive of in any season. Except for parental and pack situations, animals do not share food; creatures that might encroach on their food supply are always regarded as enemies, and only weaker animals relinquish food or territory without a scuffle. Many species might feed from the same meadow or off the same carcass, but always in a hierarchy: A bear claims a road-killed deer and eats his fill; then a coyote (cautiously) strips off chunks of remaining meat; then opossums and birds clean the skeleton, while squirrels and porcupines gnaw the bones to obtain nutrients.

This wolf-killed calf represents a puzzle to the tracker: The three wolves that brought down the calf were chased off by the farmer, and its carcass was later fed upon by coyotes, crows, and turkey vultures.

Dead animals with flesh still on their bones should never be approached (use binoculars), and the more fresh a kill appears, the greater a tracker's caution should be. Historically, wolf packs have backed off from kills to allow starving humans to feed, but large cats can be very possessive of prey, and bears are likely to charge in defense of a carcass. After eating their fill of a large animal, most large predators will partially cover it with scraped-up forest debris and dirt, a sure sign that the owner is close by, and means to return.

An interesting habit among hunting carnivores is the way the animal claiming a carcass will often mark the remains with a nearby scat as a territorial claim, and probably an advertisement of hunting prowess. Weasels, especially wolverines, are known for scenting unfinished remains with foul-smelling musk that makes the meat unpalatable to other carnivores, and cats sometimes spray large, partially eaten carcasses for the same reason, usually on a place they do not intend to eat, like the skin.

Mating Behaviors

Most species have fixed mating seasons that occur at the same time, over the same length of time, each year. Generally, these "ruts" are genetically timed to ensure that offspring grow up during the easiest season—usually summer—and most species mate in late autumn or early spring (depending on gestation period). Some animals, like bears, mate in summer, but females carry embryos in suspended animation (stasis) until denning in early winter, when they will either attach to their healthy mother's uterus, or spontaneously abort from a mother who is underfed or sickly. A few, like the cougar, may mate at any time of year, but, again, weather and availability of prey help dictate when a female comes into heat.

Abnormal behaviors by males during their mating seasons are a given, because males are driven by hormone-induced lust. Most species are polygamous, with males mating as many females as possible, and some, like whitetail bucks, may even forego eating during their annual fixation on sex. Trackers can use that preoccupation to good advantage, whether the prey is an elk, coyote, or gray squirrel, because an experienced trophy-sized male is never more likely to make a mistake than when his mind is on sex.

More sedate females are concerned only with birthing and rearing young, and have no interest in sex once they become pregnant (females can sense pregnancy). Because adult females spend most of their lives pregnant or raising offspring, it behooves them to keep a low profile. While males employ ostentatious signals that attract attention to their availability, females communicate their readiness through the use of usually urine-based pheromone calling cards left at strategic scent posts. Interested males must pursue females as they continue to feed heavily in preparation for pregnancy.

Bedding Behaviors

Most animals are "crepuscular," being most active at dawn and dusk, when they move between feeding grounds and secluded bedding places. Most species are also nocturnal, feeding primarily at night, because night has become the safest time, when humans on foot are not likely to be encountered in the backcountry, and vehicle traffic is most visible. This means that most animals go into denning places at dawn, and sleep until the cool of sunset awakens them to feed.

Herbivores that must sleep in the open tend to rely on the safety of a herd, but solitary species seek out secluded, close places for their beds. Bears, cats, hares, and coyotes are among game species with solitary lives and a preference for overgrown sleeping areas. The ideal bed is one that conceals its owner from sight and smell, where even soft-footed predators make noise when they walk, and in a location where strong winds cannot reach. Game trails through overgrown bedding places tend to be fewer and more heavily traveled, used by numerous species, with less-obvious trails branching off to bed sites.

Trails leading from feeding areas to beds are very good places to ambush any animal that uses them for daily travels. Hiding along a well-used trail at the edge of a bedding thicket is a good tactic for catching animals coming in to bed each morning, and it's a good bet that the same animal will return along the same path to feed the following evening.

When stalking a bedding area, do everything slowly, and never take a step until your eyes are certain that no animal is lying motionless in shadowed underbrush. The animal you seek is consciously hiding, and instantly awakened by odors and sounds that are out of place. Happening on a sleeping bear or moose at close range can be dangerous, needless to say.

Scents in Behavior

While many animals can vocalize their desires and intent, most communication in the animal world is

This curious squirrel trail proves that even small animals are not dumb; this narrow, regularly used trail is an escape route that lets small animals run through it at full speed, while larger predators like coyotes cannot.

This deer bed of pressed-down grasses is in a place where the animal feels safe enough to sleep, and possibly feed at the same time. Left unmolested, it will return there night after night.

accomplished through odors. No sense develops without purpose, and the more refined the sense, the greater its importance to the owner. Like radar, sense of smell is an early warning device for detecting and identifying hazards before they become immediate dangers, at ranges beyond those of vision and hearing.

Urine is an olfactory biography of its maker, carrying in it smells that identify the individual, its gender, age, strength, health, sexual readiness, and probably more. A lynx knows the boundaries of a neighbor's territory because it can smell them from a distance; a rutting buck knows how many does have visited a scrape since his last visit, and can follow any one of them; a turkey vulture—the king of smellers—can detect carrion from a range of ten miles.

A tracker must understand and abide by the rules of smell he cannot perceive. Being upwind of an animal will probably cause it to detect you from beyond sight. Leaving bodily secretions or

Nearly all animals "see" a world that is invisible to humans through an enhanced sense of smell (olfactory system).

excretions—including sweat—on any object within sight of a game trail can cause that section of trail to be abandoned for several days. In subfreezing weather, scents dissipate slowly and weakly; in hot weather, smells spread strongly, but fade quickly, sometimes within a day.

Body Language

An animal that encroaches on another's territory, past its scented boundaries, vocalizations, and visual signs either has nothing to fear from the claimant, or believes itself strong enough to appropriate that territory. Animal strangers of the same species are never welcomed kindly, but before a bloody kicking and biting match erupts, combatants square off with adversarial posturing. Violence could mean that both are bleeding, possibly blinded or broken, so actual combat is rare, and usually unnecessary.

A working knowledge of wildlife body language is critical to trackers, because they are most likely to meet an animal face-to-face on its own turf. Most large carnivores accord humans the respect due any dangerous species, and are quick to withdraw, but knowing how to interpret an animal's posturing can be essential for getting out of a stand-off unscathed.

Any wild animal that is facing you probably knew you were coming, which means that it has stood its ground for a reason. It may have something worth protecting—like offspring, or a fresh kill. A steady stare is always a warning to back off. Some experts recommend that you avert your eyes, so as not to seem adversarial, while a few experienced woodsmen claim that you should never show submission by shifting your gaze. The experts are unanimous in their opinion that a person should never run, because that incites every species to give chase.

Remain fully erect during any face-off with a wild animal. Kneeling before a black bear is perceived as a sign of aggression, while kneeling before a gray wolf is an act of submission. Spread your jacket open and make yourself look as large as possible as you step backward the way you came, never turning your back until the animal is out of sight. Make no sound so long as the animal remains motionless, but shout loudly and forcefully if it charges, because most initial charges are only a test of resolve.

It also helps to look at body language from an animal's perspective: A camper who throws a hot dog to a "friendly" wolf is telling the animal that he, and maybe the next camper, is willing to surrender tasty food when challenged. To a moose mother, we are carnivores, whatever our diets, and no carnivore is permitted near this gigantic deer's babies. To a solitary cougar, with hunting instincts so refined that it behaves much like a house cat, a small-framed jogger who is out of breath may be seen as a slow-moving animal in distress. (Refer to Section II for pertinent information about individual species).

Escape Behaviors

Every animal that flees will head for cover, whether that is into thickets of river willow, or to the other side of a distant rise. The primary goal with every species is to first get beyond visual range of whatever caused the animal to run away. Thick vegetation is preferred, because even the most acute sense of smell can be confused by the variety of scents that exist there, slowing a pursuing predator enough to permit its quarry to escape.

But a surprised animal that dives instinctively into an almost impenetrable thicket is in reality headed straight for an established game trail, where it can flee at top speed over a clear path that it

knows intimately. It might appear that a white-tail, bear, or moose has dived into brush in blind panic, but be assured that the creature will not battle its way through tangled vegetation, where it might injure itself, for any longer than is necessary. A deer tracker who has scouted his area thoroughly enough to know the location of game trails can often take advantage of that knowledge, particularly in areas of heavy hunting pressure. By stationing himself on a well-used "escape" trail, a tracker can intercept fleeing animals that have been jumped by others.

Note, too, that few animals expend more energy running than is necessary to escape danger, and most will stop as soon as they believe pursuit

While it might appear that this deer is fleeing blindly into the brush, it is in fact heading toward an established trail where it can safely run through the woods at its top speed.

has ended. A tracker who freezes immediately on jumping an animal may find that the animal runs only until it can no longer see him, then stops to look back. Having sharper vision than most creatures, a tracker can often see the animal when it stops, even though it cannot see him.

READING SIGN

Novice trackers follow footprints; veteran trackers read sign. In fact, reading sign, defined here as following visible clues, odors, and sounds other than foot impressions, is at least as important to tracking as following hoof or paw prints. Trackers who can follow an animal's trail across rock or chest-high grass are not referencing from tracks, but from other disturbances left by an animal's passage.

Territorial Sign

Beyond the generic requirements of life, wild species tend to be adapted to specific habitats—don't expect beavers in the high desert or tree squirrels on a prairie. This criteria will universally include a source of drinking water, and every animal in an area will live at or be drawn to permanent watering holes at least daily, leaving sometimes perfect tracks in wet sand and mud.

Few animals are so compliant—or so heavy—as to leave obvious tracks like a moose, making an ability to read sign integral to the science of tracking.

This is where the tracking experience can become as scientific as you want to make it, because the more any tracker knows about his quarry, the better his chance of intercepting it. Lacking hunting-level senses, humans must substitute knowledge and intellect. Common behavioral characteristics include territoriality, and every species engages in marking the boundaries of its claimed domain against intruders that might present competition for limited food and mates.

Predators are especially prone to marking trail intersections at territorial boundaries with scats that are refreshed periodically. Predator scats are all typically cylindrical with tapered ends, and distinguishable from herbivore scats by a spiral of fur encasing sharp bones that might otherwise injure the lower intestine. Predators of various species also exhibit a marked tendency to defecate atop the stripped carcass of larger prey animals after the edible parts have been consumed.

Prey animals, defined here as herbivorous species whose reproductive capacities are matched to the appetites of predators that survive by eating them, also use scats to define their trails and territories. Herbivore scats are almost universally pellet-shaped, formed of compressed undigested plant fibers that also serve to keep the colon clean.

Unlike predators, which use scat almost as a fence to delineate claimed boundaries, prey animal scats are deposited in clusters at random points along trails. The hodgepodge placement of scats actually serves a valuable purpose for prey animals; a deer jumped by a predator will head for the cover of its bedding ground, where a maze of trails exists, visibility is limited to a few yards, and getting out of sight may require a single leap. If a predator loses visual contact with its target in this scat-strewn environment, an overwhelming scent of prey can confuse the most acute sense of smell.

Feeding Sign

Every animal must eat, and the activity must leave marks on the environment. Neatly clipped vegetation identifies the feeder as an herbivore with both top and bottom incisors, like squirrels, rabbits, and porcupines. Raggedly torn grasses and plants point to grazers that lack top incisors and must rip food free, like bison and members of the deer family. Berry plants and cherry trees that appear to be undisturbed except for lack of fruits on empty stems tell of a bear that delicately plucked them free with its surprisingly articulate lips.

This partially chewed spruce cone is evidence of tree squirrels.

Mating Sign

Females of most species play a passive role in mating rituals, advertising their availability through subtle scents, but forcing males to pursue them as they feed constantly to prepare for pregnancy. Males in breeding mode tend to do the opposite, engaging in behaviors that are intended to be high-profile. The goal is to attract the attention of as many prospective mates as possible, while simultaneously warning off competitors.

To accomplish those things, mating sign runs the gamut of senses. Bull moose bellow, lynx wail eerily, and coyotes howl. Visual mating sign includes room-size areas of churned-up dirt and ravaged undergrowth wrought by elk bulls, and "raked" spots where tom turkeys have scraped leaves and debris to bare ground. Unless it is fresh enough to be wet, or contrasted against snow, cocked-leg urinations of coyotes against trees may be undetectable by a human, but the pungent, recognizable odor of cat urine can be smelled from many yards, as can active whitetail scrapes. Most important to a tracker is knowing that the finest trophy animals go out of their way to be noticed during mating season.

Bedding Sign

Every animal must sleep, and while none sleep deeply enough to be unaware of their surroundings, all understand instinctively that lying unconscious with eyes closed is inherently dangerous. To guard themselves during vulnerable sleep periods, animals tend to locate their beds in places where sneaking up on them, or even finding them, is as difficult as possible. Overgrown swamps are ideal for rabbits that sleep concealed within dense vegetation, but desert hares find the same safety in rock cracks. Whitetails and moose prefer overgrown swamps, where always-moist soil cools their bellies during the heat of a summer day, and provides both windbreak and food during the winter months. Bears, which may make a circuit of hundreds of miles as they follow seasonal foods, tend to use whatever cover and shade is available at the time, while badgers and raccoons hole up in excavated burrows.

Sleeping habits are not the same for all species. Whitetails tend to feed and sleep within the same small area their entire lives, but black bears may range hundreds of miles, remaining in a single place only until its food supply is exhausted (or superseded by better foods elsewhere). Except for their spring denning period, wolf packs roam wherever prey is found, while coyotes prefer to stay in one location. In every instance, where an animal sleeps will not be far from where it feeds and drinks.

Bedding places are ideal for trackers, but scout them with caution. Surprising a bear or moose on its bed at close range can be dangerous. Surprising a whitetail buck or napping wolf poses no hazard, but might result in abandonment of that bed, even that area.

SCOUTING TECHNIQUES

A tracker who doesn't scout the area he intends to hunt is relying on blind luck, but fortune, as the old proverb says, always favors the prepared. The objective of scouting is to establish what animals live within your hunting area, how many of them there are, and what their normal routines might be. A tracker who knows these things is always more consistently successful at finding any species of game than one who does not.

Litmus Field:

The sudden appearance of foreign objects as small as a candy wrapper on an animal trail is often sufficient to cause every species that uses that path to choose a different route until time proves that object harmless. Wild animals grow to respectable age and size by being keenly alert to minute changes in their environments, and a Scout or tracker should always presume that potential prey is on guard.

But animals cannot read tracks; the smartest of them lack the cognitive abilities to form a mental picture of what is represented by impressions in the earth. They can all detect and communicate through odors too faint to register in our human noses, but unscented marks in the ground go unnoticed. You can use this generic animal trait to exploit your human advantage of vision with a "litmus field" or "track field," so called because it visibly highlights the passage of even mice.

Often used by Border Patrol officers, a litmus field is a broken-up patch of soil made "fluffy" enough to register an imprint of any object that presses into its soft surface. Trackers afield have always used the tip of a stick or knife, or a gardener's hand rake.

A tracker should take advantage of every pre-existing field that will take and hold the tracks of animals crossing over it; barring that, a tracker must be prepared to transform the earth to be track-friendly.

Areas spanning several yards of wet shoreline can be transformed into a track field, but probably most trackers will be concerned with narrow forested "runway" trails that appear to be used with regularity. First, remove leaves and debris covering a short section of a trail, then loosen the packed topsoil or snow, filling in existing tracks, and leaving a furrowed surface that holds a clear, accurate impression. By checking the field at least daily, ideally every few hours, noting the different tracks recorded there, then erasing the field for the next passers-through, a tracker can determine, sometimes within a day, what species of animals are in the area, their sizes and relative ages, and even individuals within the same species.

Trail Timers:

Left undisturbed, animals adopt daily routines, just like humans, because doing the same thing the same way at the same time every day maximizes efficiency, with a minimum of work. Most animals are crepuscular, or most active twice a day, at dawn and dusk, as they move between daytime bedding and nighttime feeding areas. A bear or moose that trod an established trail into alder thickets this morning will emerge from those thickets to feed this evening, probably using the same trail. The more a cold-tracker can narrow his prey's timetables to within a few hours, the shorter the time spent sitting on-station in freezing weather.

String Timers:

String timers are the simplest way to establish if and when animals are using a trail. Consisting of lengths of black medium-weight sewing thread stretched across a game trail, one end tied securely, the other wedged loosely in bark or a split twig, dozens of these basic timers fit into a pocket.

By hanging the threads at different heights, and checking and resetting them at different times, it's possible to quickly identify the species that use the trail, their number and sizes, and times at which a trophy is most likely to pass through. You can even determine direction of travel by which way the string was pulled.

When using string timers, it pays to set a dozen, at different places along different trails, and at different heights. Take care not to scent the absorbent thread with odor-bearing chemicals—including your own sweat—that may remain detectable by animal noses for months. And remember to remove all strings when you have finished your tracking.

Electronic Timers:

More complex, and accurate, are battery-operated trail timers that record the day, date, time, and direction an animal was traveling when it passed through. From basic one-event models that trip when a string is pulled free to four-megapixel camera models that photograph, or even video, animals when they break an invisible beam of light, these useful scouting tools range in price from less than $20 to more than $400.

When setting an electronic timer, take precautions against leaving your own scent or sign, but also against limitations imposed by nature, especially cold. When possible, conceal the unit out of wind and within natural cover, where freezing rains or driven snow is least likely to ice-up trigger mechanisms or occlude camera lenses. Semiconductor electronics generally have a lower temperature threshold of below zero; below that, components and circuit boards can crack, and LCD screens can be permanently damaged.

Cold Tracking

People fortunate enough to live where they track have a distinct advantage over those who must travel, sometimes hundreds of miles. A tracker who doesn't have the luxury of being intimate with his tracking area

One of the greatest tracking aids of the New Millennia is the digital trail camera, capable of shooting video, stills, recording the time and date, and even capturing images at night.

needs to employ shortcuts. First of these is a detailed map of the area, a good map compass, and the know-how to use them as a system to analyze the surrounding terrain. By knowing the needs and typical behaviors of a species, then balancing those against water sources, impassable obstacles, and other features shown on your map, you can select likely spots before ever seeing them.

Cutting sign is essential to cold tracking; if there's no sign from the species you're looking for, you're probably not in a good spot. Shorelines are always a good place to start, because most animals must drink at least once a day, especially in the morning, after a night of feeding. Tracks in wet earth identify the creatures that walked there by size, weight, and, in the case of a mother with young, gender. Well-traveled deer, bear, and other trails lead from shorelines to an animal's bedding or foraging grounds, and backtracking one of these is sure to take you closer to where an animal feels secure enough to sleep.

The secret to successful cold hunting is to employ scouting devices like litmus fields and string timers on every visible trail, then to check them at least three times a day for sign. By knowing the habitat an animal prefers (see Section Two for details about individual species), the locations of every swamp and hill, and sign of the animal being tracked, a practiced cold tracker can sometimes find the animals he is looking for in a place he's never seen before.

Cameras

One of the greatest things about the popularity of cell phones, so far as trackers are concerned, is that all of them contain digital cameras. Personal cameras have been a must-have component of trackers' field kits since the 110mm film models of the 1970s, because it can be invaluable to have a visual record of a point of interest. By photographing tracks, scats, and other sign in the field, then taking them home, uploading them to a computer, magnifying, and manipulating, you might very well see something important that you had missed while you were actually there.

One drawback to using even the best camera (the author prefers a full-size dedicated camera) is that an optical lens sees in only two dimensions. That phenomenon has an impact on this book, because while a color photo is more eye-catching, sometimes it just cannot emphasize important details that would be evident to the precise depth perception of human binocular vision in the field. For that reason, in some instances, this book uses drawn illustrations that emphasize, even exaggerate, details in, especially, track impressions.

A suitable field camera is essential, but it need not be large, complex, or delicate; this camera is virtually indestructible.

Following is a list of equipment that has proved to be essential to gathering data and getting to know local wildlife while in the field. This list should be added to or subtracted from as needed.

Tracking Kit Equipment List

Observation and Data Gathering:
> Binoculars: 8x40 roof prism.
> Camera: Digital, at least 4.0 megapixel.
> Spiral notebook, pocket size, with ink pen.

Measuring Scales:
> Tape measure: Twenty-five feet, locking tape, both inches and centimeters.
> Ruler: Six inches, flexible, inches and millimeters.
> Microscope: 25x pen type, packed inside a plastic toothbrush holder for protection.

Casting Kit:
Plaster: One pound minimum, in a sealable plastic bag.
Plastic surveyor's marking ribbon, brightly colored for marking cast locations, six feet or
> more.
Spray bottle filled with water, for spritzing an icy glaze onto tracks in snow before casting.
Plaster mixing bowl: With snap-down cover, two-cup capacity or larger.
Resealable plastic dishes, low-wall, at least four by four inches, for carrying casts.
Paper towels: Partial roll, flattened, carried in plastic bread bag, for cushioning casts in dish.
Belt knife: Five-inch blade, sharp, for loosening casts, assorted field work.
Multi-Tool, with a variety of tools, marked with a scale.

Gloves: Disposable, medical or food service type, for handling scat and other matter, four to five pairs.

Air-activated handwarmer packets (winter only).

A dozen feet of duct tape wound around a pencil.

Small tube of disinfectant waterless hand soap.

Orienteering:

Compass:

Primary: Prismatic- or lensatic-sighted map compass.

Secondary: Pocket compass, liquid-filled, worn around neck.

GPS: 12-channel, AA-powered, lighted screen, replacement batteries.

Map: USGS topographical, gridded with both Universal Transverse Mercator and latitude-longitude coordinates for use with GPS and magnetic compass.

Clothing:

Boots, winter: waterproof, rated to at least -40° F.

Boots, spring and winter hiking, waterproof, internal liner.

Boots, summer: hi-ankle, lace-to-toe, waterproof.

Socks, all seasons: Wool or synthetic oversock with acrylic liner sock.

Base layer, winter: synthetic, matched to temperatures, top and bottom.

Parka shell, all seasons: hooded, large pockets, rainproof, breathable.

Trousers, all seasons: six-pocket, ripstop weave, GI-type, dark color or camouflage.

Gloves:

Summer: leather or leather-and-fabric work gloves, preferably gauntlet-length.

Winter: shell gloves with liners.

Snowshoes, hiking: Nine by thirty, aluminum frame, crampons.

Snowshoes, heavy load: Ten by thirty-six, aluminum frame, with integral crampons.

Headnet: worn over ballcap for bug protection, glare protection, camouflage.

Equipment bag:

Daypack: 2,500-cubic-inch capacity, outside pockets, internal frame, waist belt, sternum strap, padded shoulder straps, hydration pocket.

Stuff sacks: nylon, drawstring with cordlock, colored for coding individual kits.

STALKING TECHNIQUES

A tracker who is not stealthy is probably not going to be successful, no matter what he or she is attempting to track. Broadcasting one's presence is always taboo to getting a visual on live game, and every tracker wants to move as invisibly as possible through an environment, leaving no scent or sign of ever having been there. The science of invisibility begins with learning to automatically walk in a manner that doesn't require constantly looking at your feet, but disturbs as little as possible.

Slowing Down

The first rule is: slow down. The distinctive sound of a steady bipedal walk is alarming to all species, most of which will flee, although a few larger ones have reacted aggressively in protection of prey or offspring. Squirrels and birds are notorious for announcing the presence of a human to every critter within earshot, and every animal that survives in a forest learns to heed the alarm calls of red squirrels, blue jays, and geese, among others. Wild animals seldom travel with a steady stride, but inspect nuances of their surroundings as they travel, stopping frequently to take in the sights, sounds, and smells before moving on. When actively stalking any animal to eyeball range, your speed should never exceed one hundred yards per hour.

Walk slow, walk softly, but most of all, walk where the wildlife lives, and that is most often in places where people seldom venture.

The technique is easy to learn, but takes a lifetime to master; on ground soft enough to register impressions, trackers can visually gauge their skill at walking Indian by the depth of their own tracks. Observing your own tracks can tell you where you step down too heavily, at what point your balance is weakest, and how smoothly your weight was transferred forward.

Stalking

Stalking is perhaps the most romanticized aspect of the tracking experience, because if a person achieves the skill to sneak up on a rabbit, or deer even some of the time, they can definitely be proud of their tracking abilities. And if you can stalk and conceal yourself long enough to snap just one poorly-focused photo with even a cell phone as proof that you did, you possess a trophy equal to anything that previous generations might have killed and mounted on a den wall.

In nearly every instance, getting a photo of, or even just a look at, a wild animal will be a Scout/stalker's only concern. Only rarely will any species of wild fauna do anything but beat a hasty retreat at the appearance of a human. Scary movies and other tall tales aside, seeing any wild animal is nearly always more cause for celebration than concern.

But for every rule there are exceptions. Following are tips for avoiding potential problems before they occur, and for handling oneself with different species in some of the most common confrontations.

The point of stalking is to catch sight of an animal before it sees you. That requires moving very slowly—experts recommend no faster than one hundred yards per hour—and scrutinizing everything that you can see. Objects that seem out of place and unidentifiable should be more closely studied through binoculars, until a stalker knows what they are. And never, ever approach a partially-eaten carcass, particularly if the flesh looks fresh and moist.

Don't expect to see an entire animal, but look for an ear that is wiggling to shake off biting flies; or maybe a leg among the ferns; or an eyeball in a motionless head as the animal also studies its environment, alert for danger. If an animal is alert and unmoving, you should do likewise, freezing in place until the animal goes back to what it was doing or leaves the scene; there is a good chance that it isn't sure of your presence.

Whether or not a tense meeting with an animal that does not flee at the sight of you escalates into a physical encounter or ends with a peaceful parting of the ways may depend entirely upon how you react to the animal's messages. In every case, with every animal, it is an imperative that you defuse the situation before it escalates. Once an animal's fighting blood rises—the equivalent of blind fury in a human—its fear diminishes, and physical violence is almost guaranteed.

One of the best tie-breakers in a stand-off with any animal is standard equipment for many hikers, and that is a walking stick. A walking stick swung hard through the air, not at the animal (this is important), but off to one side, makes a whooshing sound that's alien and scary to every wild animal.

Humans are the only species that can adapt objects from the environment, such as rocks and clubs, to serve as weapons, and this ability alone seems frightening to animals. The effect of a stick whooshing through the air has been observed on several species of both wild and domestic animals, and in every instance the sound has proved frightening to the subject.

It is essential that you bear in mind that different species react differently to body language and vocalizations. For instance, crouching low and backing away is seen as a sign of submission to wolves. Wolves have never in history attacked a live human, or eaten a dead one, and curled lips showing fierce-looking canines are usual when a wolf feels threatened.

Crouching low before a bear, however, is perceived by the animal as a readiness to fight. Authorities agree that the best strategy when facing a bear is to stand upright and to make yourself look as large and unafraid as possible. Methods of doing so include holding a large cloth over your head to make yourself look taller, or holding the sides of a jacket open to make yourself look wider. Except for the midsummer mating season, when hormones run high, bears, especially black bears, are generally peaceful creatures. Exceptions are mothers with newborn cubs (cubs-of-the-year), and when brown bears, particularly, have a meal to protect. Again, never approach a dead animal, especially if it looks red and fresh, but use binoculars to get a closer look; there's a very good chance that a predator has possession of it and is close by.

Some professionals have recommended that you avoid looking an animal in the eye, but more recent information indicates that doing so identifies you as a weaker prey animal. It is now suggested that you maintain eye contact, identifying yourself as a dominant predator and a dangerous adversary. Never turn your back on an animal in challenge mode, and absolutely never run away; to run excites the chase instinct in every predator, and there are only a few small animals that can be outrun by a human. The almost inevitable result of running from even a raccoon is that you will be caught and mauled. And any blood drawn from you by a wild animal almost invariably results in preventative treatment for rabies.

Should an animal actually charge, stand your ground. It's easier said than done, but show no fear. Shout loudly, wave your arms wide, and swing your walking stick. This last-ditch effort to deter an animal that appears to be actively bent on doing you harm has often worked to call an attacker's bluff. All species are reluctant to engage in a physical confrontation that might injure them severely enough to hamper their ability to forage, hunt, and defend their territories. Pepper spray is a favorite attack-stopper, but you need to hit the animal square in its face, and it doesn't always stop every species.

If deterrents fail, and you find yourself in a fight with an animal, how you respond depends on the animal. A moose or elk (rarely, even white-tailed deer), especially during the autumn rutting (mating) season may rear up and try to pummel you with its hooves. In this instance, run, not in a straight line, but erratically, until you reach at least one tree about ten inches in diameter—large enough that it can't be pushed over by a half-ton animal. Keep a tree between you and those flailing hooves, and your attacker might well give up. If the animal is a moose, be patient and be cautious, because moose are notorious bushwhackers; they hide nearby and wait for another opportunity to charge.

If the attacker is a black bear or puma (mountain lion), fight back with everything you have—rocks, sticks, a knife, or anything that can inflict pain. These species are often easy to discourage, and if you hurt them, they may run away.

A brown bear is different. Using a pepper spray or weapon is likely to just infuriate the bear. Authorities have long recommended just lying down and playing dead. Expect to be mauled and bitten, but in a large number of cases you will survive if you can just lie still and convince the bruin that you're dead.

In fact, your chances of being attacked, or even confronted, by a wild species while tracking one is minimal; you're more likely to be caught in an avalanche. So use common sense and practice being aware of your surroundings—the military terms that situational awareness—and you'll find the wilderness to be a safe, enjoyable, and infinitely interesting place in which to spend time.

Camouflage

Trackers have always sought to hide themselves from sight by using natural camouflage. Early Native Americans often wore the pelt of an animal they were hunting as a ruse. Half a millennium after its invention by Scottish game wardens, the tattered-cloth "ghillie suit" is a standard among military snipers. Today, those are joined by computer-designed digital camouflage, even fluorescent orange. All of them can help, but none are perfect.

What Animals See

Most mammals are color-blind in comparison to humans, viewing their world in varying shades of blue. This is not a weakness, but a trade-off; typically, there is little advantage in seeing bright infra-reds during the day, but nocturnal species have a vital need to see at night, in the ultraviolet spectrum. Their eyes have physically evolved to see in darkness, with color-detecting "cone" cells in the eye being greatly outnumbered by light-detecting "rod" cells. Conversely, eagles, bees, and other species that have the sharp color discrimination to precisely hone-in on food are active only during daylight hours.

Blaze or fluorescent orange is a color that many hunters are legally bound to wear for safety reasons. New hunter orange is very obvious because it fluoresces with UV, glowing with an ambience that is visible to all eyes until twilight, after which it radiates especially well to animals. UV-killer detergents help to tone down blaze orange, and some deer hunters stifle the brightness of new garments by literally kicking them around on a gravel road until they appear faded.

Stalkers, especially, need to be constantly aware that even the most near-sighted animal is acutely sensitive to motion at ranges beyond their visual clarity—a deer that cannot tell what you are may flee because you slapped a mosquito. Like most creatures, mammals visually register their surroundings sixty times per second, and slow movements trigger much less of an alarm than fast, jerky motions that resemble the actions of a hunting predator.

Stalking Under Observation

Open spaces even the odds that an animal will see you if you try to approach. One proven strategy is to approach on all fours from downwind in meandering fashion, as if you were just another grazing animal. Weapons, cameras, and binoculars may drag along the ground for two hundred yards or more, so prepare them for the trip with cases and lens covers. Use tall grass, shrubs, whatever cover is available, to hide your profile, and stop frequently, as if feeding.

The Stump Method

Grazing herbivores can also be stalked using the Stump Method. This technique is based on an assumption that herbivores, especially, keep their heads down, and vision obscured, for about five seconds before raising up to look about. By exploiting a deer's lack of visual clarity and distance perception, a stalker leaving cover can use those seconds to crawl a few feet closer before freezing. When the deer (or rabbit, or marmot) looks up again, it may see your form, and might even scrutinize you for several minutes, but if you remain still, it will go back to feeding, giving you an opportunity to approach a few more feet. With practice, and maybe some luck, this method can get a tracker or hunter to within twenty-five yards of grazing animals.

Blowing in the Wind

A common tale of woe among deer hunters concerns the big trophy buck that came in from the wrong side and stared at them, making the hunters afraid to move. A solution that has worked nearly every time for generations is "blowing in the wind;" rather than sitting still, the hunter begins to sway gently in time with the breeze (even if there is no breeze). In most cases, a whitetail is staring at you because it isn't certain about what you are, or that you pose a danger. By gently swaying like a pine sapling in a breeze, not like a predator moving into position to strike, a hunter adds doubt in an animal's mind about his being worth concern, and camouflages the fact that he is slowly moving into shooting position with every sway. This strategy works equally well with a camera.

TRAILING INJURED ANIMALS

Hunting is a fact of life, and sooner or later, every hunter shoots an animal that runs off. Today, virtually every wound a hunting weapon inflicts proves mortal, but a natural burst of adrenaline and endorphins fired in response to traumatic injury can temporarily charge a game animal with extraordinary strength. A responsible hunter follows up every shot, even if he's sure he missed.

You don't need years of tracking experience to find runaway game, but you do need to know what to look for and how to decipher what you see. Wild animals are not creatures of reason, but of instinct, especially when wounded. Every whitetail is programmed to escape danger by leaping into thick undergrowth, where limited visibility and a plethora of trails, scats, and scents give it an edge over natural predators such as gray wolves and coyotes. Once a wounded animal feels safe inside the concealment of its bedding grounds, it will instinctively slow to conserve energy.

Never take your eyes off a wounded game animal in flight until it is out of sight, then mark carefully the spot where it disappeared behind cover. The animal can be counted on to lie down as soon as it feels safe from pursuit. This is an instinctive reaction meant to conserve energy until the deer recovers or expires, but prolonging life in either case.

Conversely, chasing after wounded game ensures that its fear instinct will stimulate the adrenal glands to keep its body running. A time-honored rule of thumb here is to pour yourself a cup of coffee or otherwise sit still for the next ten minutes. Because virtually all wounds inflicted by modern hunting projectiles are ultimately fatal, it's likely that your deer will travel only a short way out of sight before expiring in a concealed place. But only if it isn't startled again before its strength is gone.

After ten minutes, walk to the point where you last saw your deer, following the same path your bullet or arrow took. Search carefully the place where you believe the animal was standing when you fired. In grassy places, the most recent and most violent passage through the blades will be represented as the spot where blades are most crushed. The same applies to displaced dirt and gravel in open areas. Places where ground plants are crushed and wet indicate where the animal was standing when it fled, and twisted grasses show which direction it headed. When you locate this starting point, look for wet blood, tufts of detached hair and hide, and bits of rib bone and lung that confirm a solid hit. Bleeding is usually a good sign for the hunter, but fatal wounds sometimes bleed little, so lack of a blood trail is no cause to be discouraged.

One sometimes useful trick for locating blood spots on dead sawgrass and other terrain that hides them is to mist the trail with a pump-type spray bottle filled with ordinary hydrogen peroxide. The peroxide does no harm to the environment, but foams white on contact with blood.

Fleeing game will always take the shortest route to cover, but all rely on established trails for high-speed escape and ease of travel within thick cover. Regardless of where it enters that cover, every creature can be expected to head for an established route rather than crash headlong through untracked brush.

As you enter the woods, expect to see many tracks, some days, even weeks, old. The prints left by your animal are among them, and in fact, on top of them. The clearest, most sharply-edged impressions, identifiable because they overlay all other tracks, belong to the animal that passed by most recently. The fresher a track, the sharper its corners and the more pressed-down will be the foliage at its bottom, while the opposite is true as a track fades with age.

While every tracker needs to recognize footprints, most tracking is accomplished by following disturbances left by an animal's passing, known collectively as "sign," and wounded creatures, especially deer, tend to leave clear sign: An uneven gait with sideways slide-marks indicates the animal was unsteady on its feet. Hair left on a rough-barked tree shows where a bear staggered against its trunk. Heavy twin scrape-marks in the moss covering of rotting fallen logs mean a slipped hoof, uncharacteristic of a healthy, nimble whitetail.

It isn't uncommon for a shot animal to expire on the trail, but deer species, especially, are renowned for making a final, powerful leap into storm-felled timber or other dense cover. If you suddenly lose your animal's trail, stop where it seemed to disappear and look closely for especially deep hind

Cougar prints.

tracks that indicate a powerful jump. An adult whitetail can leap twenty feet or more, but wherever the hoofed, heavy-bodied animal touches down, it must leave some mark on the environment. If you lose the trail, don't give up; return to the last identifiable track or sign, and comb the brush with radial sweeps, beginning with a search radius of about ten yards out from that point. Look closely as you walk for mounded shapes in the undergrowth that seem to be out of place, and be especially alert for a contrasting white underbelly.

If the first sweep yields nothing, extend the search radius another ten yards; less if the underbrush is very thick. Continue covering the area in ever-widening circles, and you'll almost certainly find any downed animal within them. Deer hunters should be mindful of a wounded whitetail's tendency to make a wide circle (about one hundred yards) that brings the deer around behind its pursuer. Many a hunter has followed a whitetail back almost to the point where it was shot before recovering its carcass—this is more likely if the deer is immediately pursued.

This photo is typical of a human footprint on forest humus (even with an aggressive lug-soled boot), showing that most weight comes down on the rear of the heel, then rolls straight forward to the toe. Look closely and note the disturbed, displaced, and flattened-down pine needles and duff that indicates heave weight being pressed against them.

Our species' best sense is vision, but don't discount your senses of hearing and smell. A wounded deer, particularly one hit with a firearm, will likely have ruptured internal organs, and the powerful aroma of bowel and blood that every successful hunter knows may be carried on the breeze. Listen for the reflexive thrashing of a fallen deer's legs, which may continue to spasm for a half hour after the animal has actually died. Although ours are less acute, we have the same senses as other predators, and they can be used to good advantage in heavy cover.

If you should lose the trail and can't find it again, you can often rely on other animals to locate downed game for you. Vultures, ravens, and crows are always alert for an easy meal, but most birds lack the tools and strength to tear through tough hide. Instead, they've learned to circle directly over dead or dying animals, attracting coyotes and other scavengers that will eat their fill, but still leave plenty for the birds. This symbiotic relationship can also be used to good advantage by a confounded sport hunter who draws back several hundred yards, and observes the sky over the vicinity of where his prey fled.

TRACKING HUMANS

At some point it might become necessary to read the tracks and sign of our own species, including lost children or hikers or wayward campers How well you can follow the clues left by another person's passage through an area might well become a deciding factor in whether a lost child gets tucked into bed by her parents that night or perishes from exposure.

Humans have been denied the olfactory (smell), hearing, and other hyper-senses that almost every "lower" animal is born having, but the trade-off is that we've developed a more analytical, problem-solving brain. Unlike any other species, human trackers have the ability to visually recognize, analyze, and then mentally assemble marks made on an environment into a logical picture of what has happened there. Then we can use the picture we've assembled, and what we know about the species in general ("empirical" information, like water is wet, grass is green, and rabbits hop) to predict what a creature has done, and is likely to do in the future.

When Border Patrol agents were reinforced along the historically open Canadian border after 9/11, they soon discovered that they didn't know how to track in the dense forests of Michigan, Wisconsin, Minnesota, and Maine. This track, showing the heel at the top, is about as perfect as it gets on such terrain.

The Human Design

Being the only true biped (except birds), people have evolved distinctive and unique foot and leg structures, walking methods, and therefore tracks. Only we have legs designed to swivel freely back and forth, and even to the side. We're the only animal with a flat, elongated (plantigrade) hind foot that has a true arch. We're the only animal whose weight normally comes down on the back edge of its heel; and we're the only species whose biggest, most weight-bearing toe is on the inside, opposite every other species.

Being on Your Toes

An old expression defines readiness as "being on your toes." For example, a boxer who is on his toes is in the fight, ready to duck and weave. In other words, ready to spring into motion in an instant, just as a deer is ready to instantly take flight at the first hint of danger, or a wolf is ready to immediately set off in pursuit of dinner.

Likewise, being stealthy is described as tip-toeing. Walking normally with most body weight concentrated on the forward portion of each foot means that a minimal amount of a foot's area makes contact with the earth, and less area equals less noise being made as the creature travels. Nearly all quadruped (four-legged animals) walk weight-forward, on their toes, ready to lunge into a full-speed run, while making as little sound as possible.

But if the boxer in our example drops back onto his heels, he's tired or hurt, and not capable of moving quickly to the attack, or to avoid an attack. No boxer wants to be caught flat-footed, because that means he's less able to protect himself.

But for modern humans, being flat-footed is more or less normal, and being on our toes is unnatural and exhausting. Animals who are flat-footed and incapable of running fast include porcupines and skunks; but as you know, these species have been compensated by nature with very potent self-defense weapons.

Humans normally leave comparatively obvious, full-length tracks when they walk, deepest at the heel, where a foot comes down, then rolls forward, pushing soil rearward. As a foot travels forward, its arch makes little or no contact, then digs in again at the inside big toe, where it pushes off, leaving ground debris piled at the ball of the foot. As most hikers know, the way we walk manifests itself as a callus on the outer heel, and, especially, on the outer side of their big toes, indicating where most friction is applied.

This person is trying to be quiet, purposely walking with most body weight forward, on the toes, to make as little contact with the earth, and as little sound, as possible.

This footprint shows that its maker was dragging a foot, scuffing up the leaves (or whatever forest duff, sand, or gravel might be on the ground) ahead of the track, an indication that the maker was tired or injured.

This is a difficult print; it angles from the lower right (heel) to the upper left (toe); look very closely at the outline made by the wearer's hiking boot, and the flattened sand under the boot sole.

Walking Indian

Foot placement is critical to walking quietly. A tracker needs to move like an animal, carefully placing each foot before gently pressing its sole against the ground. Hips and knees should be loose and slightly flexed, never stiff, to absorb the shocks of walking across uneven terrain. Called "walking Indian" (by Native Americans themselves), each step forward lands gently on the outside edge of the heel, toes pointed slightly (about fifteen degrees) outward, to maximize stance, traction, and balance. As body weight is smoothly transferred forward, the supporting foot is rolled along its outer sole, ending when all weight is distributed against the ball of the foot and the toes, and the opposite foot is poised to land, outer-heel first. This stride presents your body weight to the earth over the broadest area, minimizing downward pressure, and pressing debris softly against the earth with as few crunches and snaps as possible.

The beauty of walking Indian is that it is a universal stalking technique for all types of terrain, at all speeds. At a very slow stalking pace in thick cover, this system has proved effective against even bobcats. But it isn't practical to stalk everywhere, and you can also learn to walk Indian at faster paces. With practice you can learn to walk established trails in near silence at near-normal speed, and that alone is an effective stalking strategy.

Walking Indian means to bring your forward foot down toes-outward (duck-footed), to land on the outside of the heel. As your foot rolls forward, your body weight transfers smoothly from the outer heel to the big toe. This forces you to step a bit higher than normal, clearing fallen branches, low hummocks, and entanglements, so

This footprint depicts a tracker's left foot as he "walks Indian;" note that the heel comes down most heavily on the inside (lower) edge, then rolls lightly, disturbing little, toward the outside big toe, making as little sound as possible.

that you don't have to watch your feet so much. Rolling the foot, out-to-in, as you walk distributes body weight more evenly as you move forward, causing twigs that might otherwise snap underfoot to simply be pressed soundlessly into the soil.

Another advantage of Walking Indian is that it leaves only a faint imprint, compared to a normal heel-toe walk. Minimal impact and stealth make this the preferred stalking mode of trackers and hunters everywhere.

Aging Tracks

Many of the same phenomenon that are common to animal tracking also hold true when tracking humans: The fresher the track, the more defined it will be. Corners impressed by heels and outsoles are sharp when fresh, becoming less defined with age. Grass blades and ground plants that have been flattened under a bearer's weight spring back up, slowly regaining normalcy, and eventually erasing signs that they've been stepped on. Prints pressed down into sand and damp soil become more rounded as time passes.

How much time passes before a track's characteristics become blurred, then finally erased altogether, depends on environmental factors. In warm weather, when plants grow best, elapsed time before they recover from being crushed is lessened, while in cold weather, the plants might actually turn yellow and die. A track made in mud just before a winter freeze might remain sharp and fresh-looking for months. A print left in rain-wet sand often takes a perfect track, but its defining characteristics become indistinct, and may disappear entirely in hours, under a hot sun, and especially with a wind blowing. And of course another fresher track on top of a track that you're following is always helpful for determining age.

This photo depicts a person whose track shows that he changed direction by spinning on his toe to the right; note the pine needles piled to the right, denoting that fact.

The above characteristics are universal, but within them are a multitude of variables, caused by differences in environment; factors, like humidity, temperature, and air movement. How fresh or aged a track appears is dependent on all of these, and how well all of them are used to determine how old a trail might be is a measure of field experience in various environmental conditions.

Reading Human Sign

As with trailing an animal, much of tracking a human doesn't involve following tracks at all. Remember, everything that moves on the earth leaves some sign of its passing. A body moving through tall grass cannot help but leave a furrow of blades bent away, but pushed in the same direction that the body was moving. Rain- or dew-wet grass emphasizes the passage of a body or feet because water droplets clinging to the blades help to weigh them down, but even dry knee-high grass can hold evidence of a trail for half a day or more.

Leaf litter atop a forest floor is faded on top, darker on its underside, and few people can move across that surface without disturbing it. A freshly snapped twig on the ground is lighter-colored at its broken ends than an aged one. Likewise, a twig snapped off by a passing body is more lightly colored than those that have been there long enough to turn gray. A rock at the end of a short furrow skidded there under a sole. Dead logs may be scuffed, bark dislodged, by someone who stepped on it while crossing. Especially flattened footprints tell of a person who stood there for a while.

To track illegals, our Border Patrol uses a variety of tricks: A box bedspring dragged along a dirt road leaves a *litmus field* that clearly shows any disturbance; this method is also employed by deer and bear hunters, using hand rakes. A length of dark thread or fishing line strung across a trail, its ends wedged in tree bark, is dislodged by anything that pushes against it. You can purposely arrange natural clutter, like sticks and leaves, to become noticeably displaced by a person's passage.

Don't overlook technology. A motion-activated Trail-Cam designed to photograph or video passing animals, and the date they passed, is equally effective on humans. I've used my own to catch trespassing off-road vehicles and snowmobiles, presenting law enforcement with indisputable evidence of a law-breaker's identity.

Dirty Tricks

A person who realizes that he cannot shake a tracker will resort to whatever subterfuge he can think of. Walking atop exposed tree roots and rocks that don't take an impression is common, but leaves small scuff marks that an observant tracker can spot. Remember, losing a trail (it happens) never means that the trail disappeared.

The trick of running through a stream, immortalized in movies, might help to lose dogs, but it doesn't work to shake a tracker. Loose sand underwater can hold an identifiable impression for days. Rock-strewn riverbeds are invariably covered with algae that is not only slick to walk on, but clearly shows striated slip-marks on their mossy surfaces.

In streams that are too fast-moving to grow algae, many a pursuee has been tracked through a stream. Turn over a rock from one of these streams, and you'll see that it's lighter-colored, less stained with mineral deposits from the water. Undisturbed, small stones are relatively smoothed over time by the flow of water, and an impression from man or animal can remain in them for days.

A trick to be especially aware of is walking backward, because failing to note this could cost you. A person who walks backward has to come down on the ball of his foot, leaving an inordinately deep impression. The step ends rolling backward on the heel, also leaving an extra-deep imprint. In both imprints, soil is pushed toward the toes, instead of to the rear, as in a normal track.

Natural Routes

Actually tracking a person, or an animal, by their footprints may be prohibitively time-consuming, and not always necessary. A person who isn't being pursued, or is unaware of pursuit, tends to avoid rugged country, like wet marshes, densely thicketed swamps, and scree (loose rock). Like a wounded deer, people who are aware of being pursued often purposely go through hostile terrain, trying to shake pursuers, so it pays not to reveal yourself when you're tracking someone.

Likewise, a person who's afraid of pursuit avoids open country, while someone who's lost, and hoping to be found, maintains as much visibility as possible.

A behavior common to both those who do and don't want to be found is the "over-the-next-hill" syndrome. An individual who is fleeing, as well as one who wants to be found, often surmises that climbing atop a ridge or hill will provide a vantage point. Most times, it does not, but climbing hills does expend energy unnecessarily.

SECTION TWO

HOOVED ANIMALS

Domain: Eukarya

Kingdom: Animalia

Phylum: Chordata

Class: Mammalia

FAMILY CERVIDAE

The Family Cervidae, or Deer Family, are ungulates (hooved animals) of the Order Artiodactyla (hooved animals with an even number of toes). All cervids have a split hoof, which is actually a pair of modified, heavily nailed toes in front and a pair of smaller toes, called dewclaws, located slightly above them at the rear of the foot. All species leave a split-heart shaped track, and dewclaws may print behind the hooves in softer terrain like snow, mud, or wet sand. All deer are herbivores, and none have upper incisors, only a hard upper palate that causes them to rip food plants loose by pinning them between lower teeth and palate and tearing stems free. All have an efficient digestive system that can extract nutrients from rough vegetable fibers, and only caribou are known to migrate more than a few miles.

All males, and a small percentage of females, grow antlers in early spring. Antlers are covered with "velvet," a thin skin that nourishes antlers until they mature in October, and is then shed by rubbing against trees. Polished antlers are used in ritual mating battles. Essentially shoving matches, few serious injuries result from these battles; the objective is to push an opponent's head to the ground, whereupon the vanquished contender will withdraw.

Cervids are reproductively geared to lose at least half of their populations every year. All members of the deer family, primarily the young, the old, and the sickly, are preyed on by wolves, pumas, bears, and occasionally a large bobcat or pack of coyotes, and cervid reproductive rates have evolved against them to match losses with increases.

Whitetails in particular have learned to regard suburbia as a safe haven. The upsurge in whitetail numbers since the 1940s has been followed by a susceptibility to diseases, like Bovine Tuberculosis, Chronic Wasting Disease, and probably Bovine Spongiform Encephalitis (Mad Cow Disease).

New World Moose

The largest member of the deer family, the American moose is the same animal as the elk found in northern Europe and Russia. It was misnamed after the first explorers to the New World applied that name to the first really large deer they encountered, the wapiti. The wapiti was thereafter known as the American elk, while the true American elk became known as the moose.

This three-year-old bull moose with budding antlers still in velvet is feeding on grasses, horsetails, and asters in a damp ditch.

This bull moose in full autumn antlers is preparing to take one or more mates. Photo courtesy of USFWS.

Taxonomy:

Kingdom: Animalia
Phylum: Chordata
Class: Mammalia
Order: Artiodactyla
Family: Cervidae
Subfamily: Odocoileinae
Genus: Alces
Species: Alces alces

Geographic Range:

In North America moose are found throughout the northern United States bordering Canada, through-out southern Canada and into Alaska, and downward along the Rocky Mountains into Colorado.

Habitat:

Moose prefer forests with plenty of water nearby. Pines offer year-round protection from driving winds and snow, while river willows, elkslip, and other aquatic browse can usually be found in abundance along riverbanks and shorelines. The winter browsing of moose herds, which includes softwood bark and conifer buds, can negatively affect the regrowth of those trees in places that have been clearcut for timber.

During the biting fly and mosquito hatches of spring and early summer, moose tend to migrate to higher elevations where rivers and ponds are swollen with melting snow, and stronger breezes keep biting insects from landing on a victim.

Moose winter close to the same areas they summered in, moving only as conditions demand to

 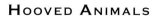

find a location that offers protection from weather, an ample supply of food until spring, and water. Mountain moose move lower to protected valleys, and forest moose gravitate toward secluded beaver ponds and floodings where spring-fed inlets never freeze entirely and there are willow twigs and bark to feed on.

Physical Characteristics:

Mass: 1,400 pounds or more at maturity. Cows roughly 10 percent smaller than bulls.

Body: Shoulder Height five to six feet. Body length eight to ten feet from tip of nose to tail. Horselike body with long legs, thick rump, and broad muscular back. Bulls carry palmated antlers from early spring to the following winter, when old antlers that can span more than four feet across are shed and new ones begin to grow.

The face of a moose is distinctive, with a long thick muzzle, a big overlapping nose, and large drooping lower lip. A fold of loose skin, called a dewlap, hangs beneath the jaws of mature males, becoming more elongated as its owner ages. Large, normally erect ears are prominent and pointed. Moose have excellent senses of smell and hearing, but their vision is nearsighted.

Tail:

Thin and inconspicuous compared to other deer, similar to that of a domestic cow but shorter, with a length of about eight inches.

Tracks:

Moose tracks are easy to locate and identify on most terrain. Being very heavy and having a hard hoof, they tend to leave clear tracks in packed soil. The split-heart-shaped hoofprint is similar to that of the whitetail, and unlike the more circular and concave wapiti track, but the hooves are twice the size of a large whitetail's, measuring four to five inches long, seven to eight inches if dewclaws are included in measurements. Moose walk weight-forward, like all deer, and on hardpacked dirt roads or trails only the foremost portions of hooves leave an impression, resulting in shorter tracks that can be mistaken for those of a whitetail.

Moose tracks.

Scat:

Normal moose scat is typical of the deer family, consisting of packed brown pellets that are usually egg- or acorn-shaped, ranging in length from one to almost two inches, or twice the size of a whitetail or mule deer. Variations in moose scat occur with changes in diet, with masses of soft manure that resembles cowpies when an animal is making the spring transition between eating bark and woody shrubs to green succulents.

Various forms of moose scat.

A unique scat configuration is the somewhat mushroom-shaped dropping that appears most common in moose that have fed on long-fibered grasses. No other animal has a scat like this one, and finding a mushroom scat is proof of a moose having been there.

Coloration:

Short fur, dark brown, becoming grizzled (interspersed with gray) as the animal ages.

Sign:

Moose leave identifiable marks on the environment where they live. The paths they plow through willow and dogwood browsing thickets are obvious from the way even larger shrubs have been pushed aside by a tall, massive body to form a V-shaped trail. Shrubs and plants at trailside are often broken and uprooted when bulls begin practicing with their antlers in late summer and early autumn, and there may be scraps of discarded antler velvet in evidence at these places. Moose beds and mud wallows are identifiable as horse-size impressions of plants and soil that have been compressed under massive weight. Moose entry and exit points into mucky bogs, where they feed on aquatic plants, are marked by a wide trough.

The most obvious winter sign of moose (and elk) are gnawings in the smooth bark of poplar, aspen, and young birch trees that serve as winter foods. These trees are heavily scarred in large areas of ten inches or more, becoming scabbed over with rough black bark as the wound heals.

Vocalizations:

Like most wild creatures, moose are generally silent. A cow calling for a calf issues a soft lowing sound, like the mooing of a domestic cow. A cow mother may also emit a sharp huffing grunt to warn intruders that they've approached too closely. During the autumn mating season, moose become more vocal, especially amorous bulls. During the rut males are loudly boisterous and virtually fearless, and have been known to charge people, livestock, automobiles, and at least one railroad locomotive. Bull moose in heat may grunt like hogs, or huff and bellow like domestic bulls. More vulnerable cows and calves communicate more quietly.

Lifespan: Ten years in the wild, up to twenty-seven years in captivity.

Diet:

An adult moose requires about ten pounds of plant material every day. Like all ruminants, moose have an efficient digestive system that allows them to process and use rough vegetable fiber as food. During summer, moose replace fat burned during the previous winter, and are most often found near open water. Browse from the shorelines of lakes, beaver ponds, and slow rivers includes pond lily, water lily, marsh marigold, horsetail, and rough grasses, and moose in Michigan's Upper Peninsula have been observed eating quantities of jewelweed (Impatiens capensis) tops, a plant known best as a remedy for poison ivy. Moose swim well, but their long legs also permit them to wade through deep muck, where preferred water plants grow thickest. In winter moose eat a rougher diet consisting primarily of willow twigs, poplar, and aspen bark. The long legs permit wading through snows too deep to be negotiated by shorter deer.

Mating Habits:

Sexually mature at two years. Mating occurs from September through October, with cows remaining in heat for about thirty days, or until pregnant. Cows initiate the rut by giving off strong sexual pheromones in their urine, and from tarsal glands inside the knees of the hind legs. Cows moo more frequently while in heat, but do not pursue mates. Male moose become extremely territorial during the rut; increased levels of testosterone cause muscles to swell, especially around the neck, and their behavior toward any intruder can be dangerously hostile.

Cow moose undergo an eight-month gestation period before giving birth to one or two unspotted calves in April or May, with twins indicating a healthy mother. If a cow is unhealthy, she may spontaneously abort the developing calf during winter, a phenomenon not unusual in nature, where offspring are more easily replaced than fertile mothers. Newborn calves are gangly, but within two days they can outrun a human, and can keep up with mother by three weeks. Weaning occurs at five months, in September or October. Wolves, bears, and mountain lions prey on calves, seeking to inflict a fatal wound to the offspring before its mother, who is too large for predators to tackle, can come to its defense. Moose calves stay with their mother for at least a year after birth, until the next spring's calves are born.

Behaviorisms:

Moose are most active at dawn and dusk (crepuscular), and mostly nocturnal. In wilder places moose may be active at all times of day, especially during the autumn rutting season. Moose bedding areas are typical of most deer, which prefer secure thickets in regularly used places where the vegetation offers plenty of concealment, and an abundance of deer scents helps to confuse a predator's nose. Whenever possible, bedding thickets will be close to or within feeding places, including dense growths of river willow, dogwoods, and poplar saplings. Adult moose are solitary creatures except during mating, when females are with calves, and on occasions when two or more may be feeding in a particularly lush spot.

Moose are generally not migratory, but in Europe, particularly Russia, moose have been known to journey as far as a hundred miles between summer and winter habitats. Strong swimmers, moose can cross swollen rivers and walk through deep snow, but normally travel alone, as opposed to migrating herds of caribou and elk.

Moose mothers are violently protective of their calves, and with a running speed of 35 miles per hour they present a danger to even large predators. Sharp front hooves are the primary weapons of either sex, although antlered bulls have used their heads, as well. Despite that, moose have been domesticated for meat and milk,

A very protective moose mother in spring with two-week-old nursing calves.

and some moose herds have been conditioned to live together in winter by handouts of hay and other food from local farmers.

Wapiti, or American Elk

A cousin of the European Red Deer, the wapiti is the second largest deer in the world. Elk were transplanted in eastern states from herds in the western US on three occasions throughout the twentieth century, after unrestricted hunting led to extirpation over much of their original range. With little fear of predators, elk make easy targets, and native populations were hunted to extinction in Indiana (1830), Ohio (1838), New York (1847), and Pennsylvania (1867) before hunting seasons and game laws were enacted to preserve remaining

A bull elk with half-grown, velvet-covered antlers, cools itself in a river on a hot July day.

herds. Unfortunately, these preventative measures came too late to save the eastern subspecies of forest-dwelling elk, *Cervus elaphus canadensis*, which is now extinct. Today elk are far from endangered, thanks to good management, and in large part to their financial value as a game animal.

Taxonomy:

Kingdom: Animalia
Phylum: Chordata
Class: Mammalia
Order: Artiodactyla
Family: Cervidae
Subfamily: Cervinae
Genus: Cervus
Species: Cervus elaphus

Geographic Range:

Wapiti were once common throughout much of the Northern Hemisphere, but today large populations are found only in the western US, from Canada through the eastern Rocky Mountains to New Mexico. A small herd of approximately nine hundred animals also exists in the Pigeon River Valley section of Michigan's Mackinac State Forest.

Habitat:

Being ruminants and browsers, elk prefer open prairies where their relatively good vision permits detection of threats by sight and scent. After centuries of hunting, the species has learned to become comfortable in forests, too. Elk have a greater tendency to migrate than whitetailed or mule deer, but only as far as is required to find a suitable habitat.

Physical Characteristics:

Mass: Nine hundred to more than 1,100 pounds. Males about 20 percent larger than females.

Body: Shoulder height of four and one-half to five feet. Six to more than nine feet in length. Stocky, more barrel-shaped than a whitetail, with muscular humps at the shoulders and flank. Hindquarters typically stand several inches higher than the shoulders, giving the elk a jacked-up silhouette.

Tail: Short, surrounded by a dark-bordered light brown to blonde-colored patch that covers most of the rump in an inverted teardrop shape.

Tracks: Four to four and one-half inches long, discounting dewclaws. Cloven, but much rounder than those of a whitetail or mule deer. Hooves tend to be concave, which results in tracks that are more deeply impressed around their outer perimeters than in the center.

Scat: Dark brown pellets, sometimes acorn-shaped, .75 to one inch long.

Coloration: Known by Indians as the "ghost of the forest," wapiti cows and bulls have a dark brown head, neck, and legs, with a

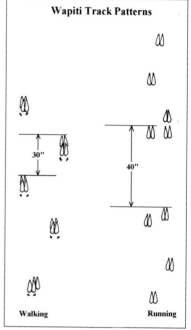

Elk track patterns.

lighter, almost blonde body that stands out when the animal is in shadows, and lends it an almost ghostly appearance during twilight hours. Both genders have a prominent blonde rump patch that provides a visual beacon for herd members to follow when running, especially calves following behind their mothers.

Sign: The most obvious elk sign is the species' signature mud wallow. These bathtub-size depressions are created by rolling in muddy earth to dislodge shed fur and parasites, or just to cool off on a hot day. Wallows can be identified by the presence of light-colored hairs and tracks in the mud within and around them.

Like moose, wapiti feed on the smooth bark of poplar, aspen, and cottonwood trees during winter months, leaving the trunks scarred with their bottom-teeth-only gnawings. As these scrapes heal over the following years, they become covered with a rough black bark "scab" that contrasts against the tree's smooth, lighter colored bark.

Vocalizations: Best known among elk voices is the "bugle" call of a mature rutting

Essentially a soft mass of pellets, this elk scat denotes a succulent diet of fresh green plants.

bull. This loud, high-pitched call, intended to be heard by receptive cows over long distances, begins as a low grunt, then abruptly becomes a hollow squeal that spans several seconds and repeats two or three times. Breeding males can also make coarse grunting and growling sounds, reminiscent of domestic cattle. These calls are heard only between elk bulls, particularly during the rutting season when they're vying with one another for mates. The alarm call used by either sex is a piercing squeal. Cowlike mooing between mothers and calves keeps them close to one another, and pairs of contentious cows box with front hooves while making softer squealing or grunting sounds.

Lifespan: Eight to ten years in the wild, longer in captivity.

Diet:

An herbivore, the elk's diet is varied enough to give it numerous food options. In summer they eat most types of grasses and forbs, marshland plants like marsh marigold, and the namesake elkslip. In winter the diet becomes rough and fibrous, even woody, including bark, twigs, and buds of aspen, poplar, beech, cottonwood, basswood, cedar, and evergreens. Elk are true ruminants, feeding on vegetation, then retiring to a resting place where the partially digested "cud" in their primary stomach is regurgitated to be rechewed and broken down further into usable nutrients. This typically cervid characteristic is also seen in bovids, like domestic cattle and bison.

Like other deer, and most animals, elk are especially active during the twilight hours at dawn and dusk. Human presence may dictate that they feed primarily by night then sleep and ruminate under cover by day, but elk that are left undisturbed tend to be daytime grazers and may spend all of their time in the same place.

Mating Habits:

Mating season for wapiti coincides with that of other deer, beginning in late August through September with a gathering of mature bulls and cows, and peaking in October and November, when the actual mating season occurs. Both genders reach sexual maturity at sixteen months, but bulls less than two years old will probably not mate due to competition from stronger males. Cows initiate the mating period by emitting pheromonal scents. A wandering bull seeking its own territory might attract young cows, thereby establishing a new herd, but more often males will travel to females. Bull elk are known for the harems they gather, but cows play a passive role in courtship rituals, and harems are usually

This handsome bull in December will be shedding its polished antlers in a few days, and another set will begin growing immediately.

maternal families consisting of a dominant female and her offspring. A typical harem consists of one bull, six adult cows, and four calves.

Like other deer, courtship battles between rutting elk are typically shoving matches in which the competing males lock antlers and attempt to shove one another's head to the ground, whereupon the weaker animal submits and withdraws. The objective isn't to harm an opponent, although injuries sometimes occur when half-ton bulls exert all of their strength against one another.

Bull elk mate with as many cows as possible, then withdraw at the end of the rut. Gestation for impregnated females lasts eight to nine months, with a single thirty-five-pound spotted calf being born in April or May. If mothers are healthy and food is abundant, cows might have twins, but this is unusual. Calves and mothers live separately from the family herd for about two weeks, and calves are weaned at about sixty days. Cows are exceptionally protective of calves. Predation by wolves and bears may occur, but few carnivores are willing to brave the sharp hooves of a protective mother elk. Male calves leave their mothers at sexual maturity, often by banishment, to prevent inbreeding that might weaken the gene pool. Females may stay with the family herd for their entire lives.

Behaviorisms:

The most social of deer, wapiti spend their lives in the company of their own kind. Except for the mating season, adults run in same-sex herds of males and females that may number from just a few to several dozen. The "bachelor" herds get along well, and commonly accept wandering strangers into their company. There is rarely animosity except during the autumn rut.

Cows are less accepting of strangers, and despite the majestic appearance of bulls, the dominant animal in every mixed-sex gathering of elk is a female. Cow and bachelor herds frequently share the same feeding and bedding areas, but the sexes do not socialize outside of the rut. If alarmed, a

Outside of the October-November mating season, bull and cow elk live separately in same sex herds, but in any herd, the dominant cow is the alpha leader.

gathering of elk will split into two distinctly same-sex herds.

Dominant cows are more territorial than bulls at all times of year, protecting their feeding areas from strange cows with flailing front hooves. Territorial battles aren't common, but the herd matriarch will protect her claimed area against any usurper, and fights are often more violent than mating contests among bulls.

Whitetailed Deer

The whitetailed deer, alternately known as the Virginia or flagtail deer, is the most popular game animal on the planet. Its value to sport hunters has spawned an industry of manufactured goods designed to get humans within shooting range. No wild animal has been more researched, mostly because no other game species is so commercially valuable.

Nearly wiped out from unrestricted hunting by the 1940s, whitetails have made a strong comeback, with an estimated fifteen million animals in the United States alone. The resurgence of whitetailed deer counts as one of our most successful efforts at wildlife management.

An adult whitetail buck with antlers in December. Courtesy of USFWS.

Taxonomy:

Kingdom: Animalia
Phylum: Chordata
Class: Mammalia
Order: Artiodactyla
Family: Cervidae
Subfamily: Odocoileinae
Genus: Odocoileus
Species: Odocoileus virginianus

Geographic Range:

Whitetail deer are common throughout the US, inhabiting all but the most arid regions, and extending northward throughout southern Canada. Their range to the south includes Mexico, Central America, and the northern portion of South America.

Habitat:

The most adaptable of deer, whitetails can live in any habitat that provides sufficient plant and tree browse, water, and concealment. They sometimes graze in open fields, but will never be far from dense cover that provides them an escape avenue from predators and a safe place to sleep. The least migratory deer, a typical whitetail will spend its entire life in an area of about one square mile, moving only between open feeding and concealed bedding places, and trackers can expect every individual to be intimately familiar with every facet of its habitat.

Physical Characteristics:

Mass: One hundred fifty to two hundred pounds, occasionally exceeding three hundred pounds in the far north. Subspecies like the key deer of Florida and the Coues deer of Arizona average fifty pounds and seventy-five pounds, respectively.

Body: Muscular and less barrel-shaped than other deer species, four to seven feet from chest to rump. Shoulder height three to four feet. Powerful hindquarters with strong, slender legs can propel them through dense undergrowth at speeds in excess of thirty miles per hour. Whitetail antlers are configured with a single main tine, or "beam," extending from the top of the head on either side, forward of the ears, from which single "point" tines extend. Antlers are shed in January and begin to grow again in April.

Whitetails and other deer have interdigital scent glands between their hoof halves that carry a signature scent and secrete alarm scents when the animal is frightened. At two years, bucks (and about one in fifteen does) grow mature, tined antlers. Metatarsal glands on the outside of each hind leg and a larger tarsal gland on the inside of each hind leg at the knee are used for olfactory communication, with musk from them becoming especially pungent during mating season.

Whitetail tracks in soft mud showing declaw imprints as round holes to the rear.

Tail: Four to five inches long, brown on top with white underside. Tail is held erect when the deer is fleeing, exposing its white underside, and giving rise to the common name "flagtail."

Tracks: Cloven hooves that leave a split-heart impression when the toes are together, two dewclaws behind and slightly above. Length: Three to three and one-half inches without dewclaws.

Scat: Typically oval-shaped pellets, sometimes acorn-shaped, 0.5 to .75 inches long, dark brown color, lightening with age.

Coloration: Reddish coat in summer, gray in winter. White chest and belly. Nose black with white band running around muzzle, white chin, white circles around the eyes.

Sign: Raggedly torn grasses. Saplings with

This fresh whitetail scat deposit shows the variety of shapes the normal pellet form can have.

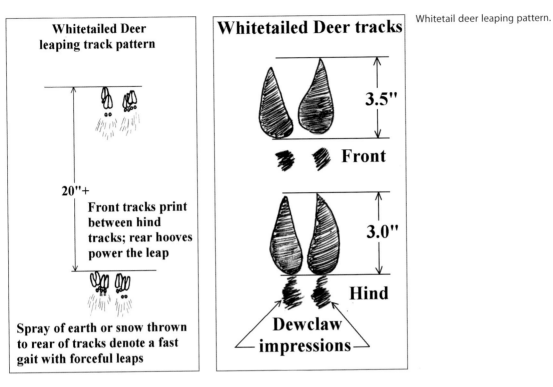

Whitetail deer leaping pattern.

Whitetailed Deer leaping track pattern

20"+

Front tracks print between hind tracks; rear hooves power the leap

Spray of earth or snow thrown to rear of tracks denote a fast gait with forceful leaps

Whitetailed Deer tracks

3.5"

Front

3.0"

Hind

Dewclaw impressions

bark scraped from them by a buck's antlers ("rubs"), seen especially in early autumn. Patches of urine-scented pawed-up earth, called "scrapes," seen during the mating season.

Vocalizations: Normally silent. Alarm call is a forceful exhalation, like a sudden release of pressurized air. Does bleat softly to fawns, but the sound carries only a few yards. Mortally wounded deer bleat with a goatlike sound.

Lifespan: Eight years in the wild; up to twenty years in captivity.

Diet:

Whitetails are generally nocturnal, with crepuscular feeding patterns, feeding most heavily during the twilight hours before dawn and nightfall, when they also visit water holes. Summer foods include all types of grasses, alfalfa, clover, elkslip, and sometimes aquatic plants. Winter browse consists of buds and tender twigs of evergreen trees, especially cedars, as well as bark and buds of staghorn sumac, river willow, beech, and dead grasses found in hummocks along stream and river banks. In more arid country they can subsist on prickly pear, yucca, and other tough, fibrous shrubs.

Mating Habits:

Mating season coincides with that of other deer, beginning in September and October with a pre-estrus rutting period during which bucks polish their antlers against young trees and advertise sexual availability with urine-scented "scrapes" of pawed-up earth. During this period adult bucks will spar with one another, usually far back in the woods, in what are essentially elimination rounds to determine which can lay claim to a territory and its females. Battles are primarily shoving matches in which contenders lock antlers and push until one withdraws. Occasional injuries result from these contests of strength, and in rare instances both bucks have died because their antlers became inextricably locked, but the intent is never to injure an opponent, just to drive it away.

Whiteails, like this doe, are widespread and adaptable.

When mating begins in mid-October, bucks will have established their territorial boundaries. From then until the rut ends in late November (December in warmer southern regions), breeding males are fixated on mating, and may be active at any time of day. Receptive does, which may mate in their first year, play a passive role, stopping only to deposit pheromone-scented urine onto a buck's scrape as they travel between feeding and bedding areas. Pregnant does need to gain as much body fat as possible to survive the coming winter, so bucks check their scrapes frequently for pheromonal messages, then pursue does who leave one.

Like all deer, whitetail bucks are polygamous, mating with as many receptive does as possible during the thirty to forty-five days of the rut. Bucks may remain with the same female for several days, waiting for her to come into estrus, but after mating, the male will move on to another fertile doe.

Does are in heat for a single day; if a doe goes unmated during her day of fertility, she will come into heat again approximately twenty-eight days later. Should this second heat pass with a doe still not pregnant, she will not come into heat again until the following October.

Gestation lasts through the following winter, with a duration of six to seven months. Does bred for the first time normally give birth to a single spotted fawn in April or May, with twins being the norm thereafter, sometimes triplets if food is abundant. Fawns are able to walk within hours after being born, and within a week begin nibbling on vegetation. Mothers leave their fawns hidden in deep grasses or underbrush while they graze nearby, checking on them from time to time and eating their feces to help prevent predators from detecting them by scent. If a carnivore should approach too closely to a hidden fawn, the mother will usually try to distract the predator and lead it in the opposite direction, but she won't risk her own life to save her offspring. Weaning occurs at approximately six weeks, but fawns remain with their mothers for the rest of the summer, and sometimes through the winter, even though their mothers are likely to be pregnant with next spring's fawns.

Behaviorisms:

Whitetails are generally nocturnal, traveling from secluded bedding areas to feeding places at dusk, then returning to the safety of dense thickets or forest at dawn. They may move about within the seclusion of these bedding areas during the day, and they may be seen grazing in the open during daylight hours, but normally avoid contact with humans.

When winter snows cover the fields and meadows, whitetails move into protected "yards" where pines and especially cedars provide windbreak and browse. In most places winter yards are the same as summer bedding areas, enabling deer to use established trails year round.

As with elk, whitetail does are the most dominant deer, and they're more territorial than bucks at all times of year because survival demands securing a habitat with enough food, water, and shelter to support them. Territorial disputes are settled with flailing front hooves, and the contests are often violent.

Whitetail deer are mostly solitary throughout the summer months, but an abundance of food, especially farm crops, can cause them to herd together in large numbers. Agriculture has caused whitetail populations to explode in farming regions where predatory species are historically unwelcome, with the result being overpopulation, disease, and an increase in car-deer accidents.

Mule Deer

Mule deer represent the second most popular large game animal in America. Subspecies include the blacktailed deer of America's northwest coast.

A mule deer herd. Courtesy of NPS.

Taxonomy:

Kingdom: Animalia
Phylum: Chordata
Class: Mammalia
Order: Artiodactyla
Family: Cervidae
Subfamily: Odocoileinae
Genus: Odocoileus
Species: Odocoileus hemionus

Geographic Range:

Mule deer are found from southwestern Saskatchewan through central North and South Dakota, Nebraska, Kansas, and western Texas, with isolated sightings in Minnesota, Iowa, and Missouri.

Gaps in their distribution occur in arid regions of Nevada, California, Arizona, and the Great Salt Lake desert.

Habitat:

Nearly as adaptable as the whitetailed deer, with whom its range overlaps, O. hemionus occupies a wide range of habitats, including California chaparral, the Mojave Sonoran desert, the interior semidesert shrub woodland, the Great Plains, the Colorado Plateau shrubland and forest, the Great Basin, the sagebrush steppe, the northern mountains, and the Canadian boreal forest. Mulies prefer open grassland for grazing, and are rarely found far back in the woods.

Physical Characteristics:

Mass: One hundred ten to more than four hundred pounds, with those in southern regions being typically smaller than those in the north. Males about 25 percent larger than females. Shoulder height is three feet.
Body: Stockier and more barrel-shaped than the whitetail, four to more than six feet from chest to tail. Very large mule-like ears, four to six inches long. Buck's antler spread about four feet. Antlers differ from the whitetail's in that the main beam forks into points, rather than having points growing individually from the main beam. Adapted to open plains and mountain country, O. hemionus has good vision, probably keener than a whitetail's.

Tail: Five to nine inches long, dark brown or black above, white below, tipped with a black or sometimes white tuft.

Tracks: Very similar to the split-heart print of the whitetail, but usually larger in adults, measuring about three and one-half inches long, discounting dewclaws.

Scat: Similar to the whitetail's, being pellet- or acorn-shaped, with individual pellets averaging about 0.5 to .75 inches long. Sometimes pellets will be massed together when browse has been succulent.

Coloration: Dark brown to red during the summer months, becoming more gray in winter. The rump patch is white in younger individuals, becoming more yellow as the animal ages. The throat patch is white. A dark V-shaped mark that is more conspicuous in males than females extends from between the eyes upward to the top of the head.

Sign: Similar to the whitetail, consisting of saplings from which bark has been scraped by bucks rubbing their antlers. Mule deer bucks make urine-scented scrapes during the rut, much like whitetail bucks. Occasionally both sexes will wallow in mud like an elk, leaving depressions that are smaller than an elk's.

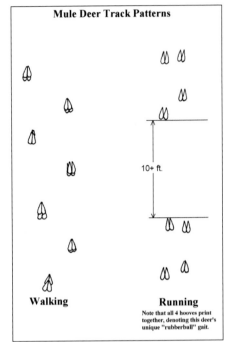

Mule track patterns. Note this species' "rubberball" bounding run, which is unique among North American deer.

Vocalizations: Alarm similar to the blowing of a whitetail, but more prolonged, and ending with a high-pitched whistle. Mule deer are more vocal than whitetails when grazing together, communicating among themselves with a variety of grunts, snorts, mooing sounds, and soft squeals.

Lifespan: About ten years in the wild.

Diet:

Although a cud-chewing ruminant like other members of the deer family, mule deer have a less efficient digestive system than their cousins, requiring more easily digestible green plants in their diet. This explains why the whitetail, with its remarkable digestive system, has expanded into the mule deer's range, but not vice-versa. To counter the deficiency of green browse in winter, O. hemionus feeds with more urgency than other deer during the summer months to put on enough fat to sustain it through winter. Green grasses, acorns, legume seeds, berries and fleshy fruits are among the preferred foods.

Mating Habits:

Mule deer breed slightly later than whitetails, with the rut beginning in October and peaking from November through December. As with whitetails, bucks create urine-scented scrapes of pawed-up earth that receptive does urinate onto as they pass between feeding and bedding areas. When the buck returns to its scrape to check for olfactory messages and finds a pheromonal calling card, it immediately sets out in pursuit. Mule deer bucks are polygynous, having more than one mate per breeding season. Bucks are known to remain with a single doe only so long as it takes to make her pregnant, or until displaced by a competitor, but there is no bond between males and females.

Bucks competing for mates engage in pushing matches by locking their antlers and shoving hard against one another until the weaker opponent surrenders and withdraws. Injuries sometimes occur, but the objective is to establish which male is the stronger, not to harm one another.

Mulie does are less likely to mate in their first year than whitetails. First, and sometimes second, births usually produce a single fawn, with twins being the norm thereafter. Gestation lasts about twenty-nine weeks, with most fawns born from mid-June to early July. Fawns weigh from six to ten pounds at birth, with twins typically weighing less than singles, and males slightly heavier than females. Fawns can walk within a few hours after being born, and begin nibbling at vegetation within a few days. Fawns are weaned by sixteen weeks, and attain full skeletal development at three years for females, four years for males, although both continue to grow until the ages of eight and ten years respectively.

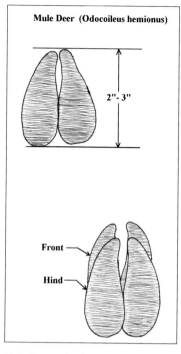

Mule deer tracks showing the split-heart cloven hoof common to all deer species, and the way hind feet are placed into front tracks during a normal, casual walk.

Behaviorisms:

Mule deer prefer a small home range that provides for their needs in every season, but they can be migratory when weather and other conditions dictate that they seek out a more suitable habitat. Bucks are driven away by their mothers at about two years of age to prevent inbreeding, and most will travel five or six miles in search of their own territories. Seasonal movements can also be prompted by hatches of biting insects, lack of water in arid regions, and deep winter snows.

Although mule deer prefer to bed down during the daylight hours in concealing thickets, they're less nervous about being in the

A buck in winter. Notice the velvet-covered antlers. Courtesy of NPS.

open than whitetails. Major predators include mountain lions and wolves, with bears and coyotes preying on fawns. By feeding and bedding in open areas mule deer can see these predators from as far as four hundred yards, and their bounding "rubberball" run of more than thirty miles per hour gives them an edge in escaping. If surprised at close range, a mule deer's powerful hind quarters and its ability to instantly change direction allows it to evade most predators.

Does are more territorial than males at all times of year, defending their home range against other does that might deplete an area's resources. Fights between contentious does are often violent, consisting of pummeling blows from sharp hooves. Bucks are spurned by females except during mating season, traveling alone or in bachelor herds for most of the year.

Mulies often run afoul of timber companies by browsing on economically important trees like the Douglas fir and Ponderosa pine, which serve as the species' winter browse. This has prompted state governments to purchase tracts of land that provide suitable winter habitat, which in its turn has created a public stir among citizens who object to their governments buying private properties.

Odocoileus hemionus is subject to a variety of viral, bacterial, and parasitic diseases. Gastrointestinal nematodes (worms) are known to cause death among them, particularly in instances of overpopulation, with resultant malnourishment. Infection by the parasitic meningeal nematode can cause fatal neurological complications, also more common in herds that have become overpopulated in relation to available habitat. Livestock may infect mule deer that graze the same pastures with viral infections like hoof-and-mouth disease (characterized by blistering of the mouth and feet), or bacterial diseases like bovine tuberculosis.

Caribou

Caribou are best known as reindeer. In fact, caribou have been domesticated to pull sleighs and wagons, as well as for their milk, and they've historically been an important source of food in arctic cultures.

Taxonomy:
Kingdom: Animalia
Phylum: Chordata
Class: Mammalia
Order: Artiodactyla
Family: Cervidae
Subfamily: Odocoileinae
Genus: Rangifer
Species: Rangifer tarandus

An adult bull caribou in early autumn; bloody tissue at the end of brow tine is a remnant of the velvet that nourishes the antlers during growth.

Geographic Range:
Historically, caribou were native to all northern latitudes, but extensive hunting by humans has made this most northern of deer extinct over much of its original range. Large herds can still be found in Alaska, Canada, Scandinavia, and Russia, and unrestricted hunting is now a thing of the past.

Habitat:
Caribou are most at home in arctic tundra, where they migrate long distances in response to changing seasons and availability of food. They can adapt to temperate forest and rainforest, but require open plains and cold winters.

Physical Characteristics:
Mass: Bulls weigh from two hundred seventy-five to six hundred pounds, females from one hundred fifty to three hundred pounds.
Body: Shoulder height: three to three and one-half feet. Four and one-half to seven feet long. Stocky build with thick legs and unusually large knee joints. Large snout and nose pad.
   Both sexes are antlered, with males having the largest and most branched antlers.
Tail: Four to six inches, darker colored on top, white below.
Tracks: Cloven hooves leave almost round impressions, four to five inches long, with males leaving larger tracks than females. The feet are slightly broader than they are long, and flat with deeply cleft hooves; this hoof design permits better stability in winter snows and spongy arctic tundra. The pad

between hoof halves is larger in summer to provide better traction against soft, slippery terrain, but shrinks in winter to help conserve heat.

Scat: Acorn-shaped pellets, about one-half inch long, sometimes clumped together in a mass that can measure more than three inches in length when the animal has been feeding on succulent browse.

Coloration: The coat is very heavy with dense, woolly underfur. Coat color is predominantly brown to olive, with whitish chest, buttocks, and legs. Coloration often varies with geography; some populations in Greenland and northeastern Canada have nearly white coats.

Sign: Browsed reindeer moss (Cladina rangiferina) lichens, a staple in the caribou diet that's seldom eaten by other deer species. Shed antlers on open tundra.

Caribous track pattern, trotting.

Vocalizations: Gutteral grunts, squeals, and whistles. Caribou are especially vocal during seasonal migrations when large groups prompt a variety of individual communications. Cows moo softly to young calves.

Caribou have thick tendons that snap across a bone in the foot when they walk, producing a clicking sound. This sound is alluded to in the Christmas carol lyrics, "Up on the rooftop, click, click, click." Trackers often use this noise, which can be quite loud in a moving herd, to locate the animals.

Lifespan: Four to five years in the wild, up to thirteen years in captivity.

Diet:

Caribou are strict herbivores that can digest most available types of vegetation, including green leaves, evergreen buds and foliage, and fine twigs. When other types of browse are unavailable, caribou may feed predominantly on their namesake reindeer moss (Cladina rangiferina), a hardy lichen that grows in carpetlike masses and is common to open, barren places around the globe.

Mating Habits:

Mating season occurs throughout October, with northern populations coming into rut earlier than those in the south. Both sexes can breed at two years, although competition from dominant bulls will likely keep males from mating until their third year. Cows are seasonally polyestrus, meaning that those not impregnated during the first ten-day period of estrus will come into heat again ten

Caribou sometimes migrate in large herds in spring and autumn.

to fifteen days later. Caribou bulls gather a harem prior to mating; harem size may exceed twelve cows, depending on competition from other bulls.

In May or June, after a gestation of about eight months, a single calf is born. Twins may occur when food is abundant, but this is not common. Calves weigh twelve to nineteen pounds at birth; they can follow their mothers within an hour of being born, and can outrun a human by the end of their first day.

Behaviorisms:

Caribou are diurnal (active during the day) and gregarious in nature, forming herds that can number from ten to more than one thousand individuals, increasing to as many as 200,000 animals during seasonal migrations. Caribou are the most migratory of deer, traveling as far as one thousand miles between northern summer habitats to more southerly winter grazing areas. Migrations happen abruptly, with smaller herds coalescing into sometimes huge herds that can number more than 20,000 animals per square mile and travel more than thirty miles per day.

Caribou are the fast runners in the deer family, able to reach speeds of fifty miles an hour for short distances, and healthy animals can quickly outdistance their most common predator, the arctic wolf. They cannot so easily escape rifles, and had been hunted to extinction over most of their European range by the 1600s, and were becoming scarce over much of their Canadian range in the twentieth century. Today there are thirty wild herds in North America; the smallest of these in Idaho and Washington, numbering about thirty animals each, while the largest in Canada and Alaska number more than 50,000. Hunting laws have helped to preserve existing populations, but oil exploration may yet prove to be a threat.

FAMILY SUIDAE

The Family Suidae is comprised of sixteen species of pigs and hogs in eight genera. Suids originally occurred across southern Eurasia, on large remote islands like the Philippines and Sulawesi, and throughout Africa. Humans have introduced Sus scrofa, the wild boar from which domesticated pigs were bred, in numerous places around the globe, including North America, New Zealand, Australia, and New Guinea. Fossilized evidence of suids has been found from the Oligocene Period (thirty million years BCE) in Europe and Asia, and from the Miocene Period (fifteen million years BCE) in Africa.

Wild Pig

For our purposes, the wild boar, feral hog, and domestic pig will be considered as a single species. The true wild boar of Eurasia is the forebear of domestic swine, but both of them share the same general behaviorisms and physical characteristics, and wild boars have been widely transplanted as game animals around the globe since before the Middle Ages. Wild boar and domestic pigs interbreed freely, and in places where both exist they've hybridized into a third type of swine that shares the markings, coloration, and other physical traits of both.

Wild pigs.

Taxonomy:

Kingdom: Animalia
Phylum: Chordata
Class: Mammalia
Order: Artiodactyla

Family: Suidae
Subfamily: Suinae
Genus: Sus
Species: Sus scrofa

Geographic Range:

Wild pigs are found throughout the world, including Pacific islands, Australia, Europe, Asia, and Africa. In many regions they were imported either as game animals or for domestication, and escaped captivity to become part of local ecosystems, sometimes with severe negative impact on native species. Of all members of the pig family, Sus scrofa, the wild boar from which all domestic pigs were spawned in approximately 3,000 BCE, occupies the largest range.

Originally there were no pigs in the Americas except the peccaries of South America, Mexico, and the southwestern US, which are not considered true swine. The first domestic pigs arrived with European immigrants, and these were not able to survive on their own in the vast wilderness of the New World; there were no feral populations until 1893, when fifty wild boar were transplanted from Germany's Black Forest to a hunting preserve in New Hampshire's Blue Mountains. These were followed in 1910–12 by a release of Russian wild boar in North Carolina, near Tennessee, and another in 1925 near Monterey, California. A few were also released on California's Santa Cruz Island.

Habitat:

Although Sus scrofa is found in a variety of habitats, the typical wild habitat consists of marshes, forests, and shrublands, where acorns, grasses, and roots are abundant. The species is poorly suited to life in deep snow, and not sufficiently furred to endure prolonged subfreezing temperatures, so wild pigs are not found in northern areas with heavy snowfall. Temperatures below 50° Farenheit are uncomfortably cold to wild pigs, although many survive in places where there is mild snowfall. Conversely, swine don't do well in hot climates, where lack of a protective coat makes them prone to sunburn and heatstroke; those that do live in warm places seek shade during the day, and wallow frequently in mud to cool themselves.

Physical Characteristics:

Mass: One hundred sixty to 450 pounds, occasionally more than 1,000 pounds; females about 20 percent smaller.

Body: Barrel-shaped, very stout; short, thick legs. Body length four and one half to six feet. Shoulder height up to three feet. Large head with short, massive neck and long muzzle ending in a flat disc-shaped snout with large nostrils. Eyes small in relation to head size.

Sus scrofa has an advanced sense of taste and a very good sense of smell. Long-range eyesight is believed to be poor. Interbreeding between feral and true wild pigs has led to a variety of ear shapes, ranging from small and erect to large and folded over at their fronts. Most prominent is the flat disc-shaped snout of tough cartilage, used for rooting in soil.

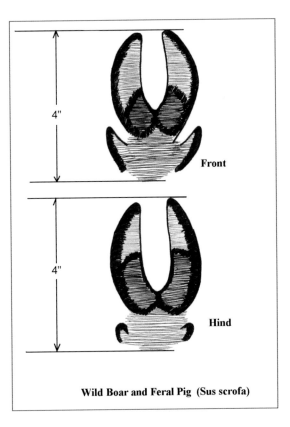

Wild Boar and Feral Pig (Sus scrofa)

Although considered an omnivore, pigs have canines that might classify them as carnivores. The upper canines grow out to curve backward into large, arced tusks that function as tools for digging and as weapons; length may range from three to nine inches, with longer tusks denoting older animals. Upper and lower canines grow throughout the animal's life, but are so closely set that jaw movements keep them honed to sharp points.

Tail: Varied, but average about eight inches. True wild boar have a straight tail with a tufted end, while domestic swine tend to have coiled tails; hybrids may have a combination of both.

Tracks: Cloven-hooved with dewclaws usually printing to the rear of hoofprints. Tracks two to four inches long, shaped like a deep U. Dewclaws in front track longer and more prominent than hind dewclaws.

Scat: Usually large pellets, similar to those of a deer, but ranging from three to more than six inches long, sometimes massed together. When the animals have been feeding on succulent vegetation or rich meat, scats may become soft and disc-shaped, like small cowpies. Recognizable content includes undigested plant fibers, insect legs and carapaces, seeds, and small bones.

Coloration: True wild boars possess a grizzled dark brown coat with whitish guard hairs that is typically longer and shaggier than that of hybridized feral pigs. Feral pigs often exhibit the splotched skin pigmentation of domestic hogs.

Sign: Well-traveled trails made by herds of foraging pigs. Rooted-up soil with grasses and roots neatly clipped free by the animals' sharp teeth.

Vocalizations: Grunting, oinking, and squealing when excited or threatened. Some researchers believe that Sus scrofa speaks a rudimentary language, but specifics have yet to be identified.

Lifespan: About twenty years.

Diet:

Swine are believed to represent a primitive condition of ungulates because they have a simple digestive system with a two-chambered stomach that processes tough plant fibers less efficiently that most hooved mammals. Pigs are omnivorous, with a diet that includes fungi, leaves, roots, bulbs, fruits, snails, insects, snakes, earthworms, rodents, eggs, and carrion. They use their tough snout, tusks, and forefeet to unearth food plants.

Sus scrofa's broad diet has enabled the species to survive in a variety of environments, from deserts to mountainous terrain, so long as winter snows are shallow enough to permit the short, heavy pigs to travel without foundering. Their herbivorous diet brings swine into direct competition with black bears, and in some states, most notably Tennessee, both species have been known to kill one another over territory.

Wild pigs aren't the gluttons they're purported to be, and are typically much leaner than farm-raised hogs. Being self-sufficient, they're more active than domestic pigs, and subsist on a less fatty diet. Like domestic swine, wild pigs are host to parasitic infections (trichinosis, cysticerosis, brucellosis) that are transmittable to humans who eat undercooked meat, and from contact with their scats,

Mating Habits:

Swine become sexually mature at eighteen months, but continue to grow until five or six years. Being herd animals, only one dominant male (boar) is permitted to breed, so most males leave the herd to find their own mates and territories at two or three years of age.

Mating season runs from mid-November to early January, peaking in December. The rut can be unnaturally violent, and large boars frequently inflict serious, even mortal wounds on one another while battling for a harem that may number up to eight sows. Extra-thick skin covering the chest, shoulders, and underbelly offers some protection against stab wounds, but fights are often bloody. Sows are in estrus for three weeks, and are receptive to copulation for about three days during that period. Females not impregnated during that time will probably come into heat again before the mating season ends. In northern regions, sows birth one litter per year, but in warmer climes breeding may take place year-round.

Gestation lasts about four months, with litters of three to sixteen (five is average) piglets being born in April. Piglets are six to eight inches long, and have brown fur patterned with nine or ten paler longitudinal stripes on the back. Sows withdraw from their herds to a secluded, defendable grass-or leaf-lined nest a day prior to giving birth. Few predators are willing to challenge a ferociously protective mother sow, but boars have been known to kill and eat their own newborn, while coyotes and larger birds of prey are quick to snatch piglets if they can. On average, only about half a litter can expect to reach maturity.

Sows rejoin their herd one to two days after giving birth, and by one week the young are able to travel with the group. The young begin feeding on solid foods almost immediately, but suckle from their mothers for three months. The piglets' stripes fade slowly, until they're completely gone at six months and the animals take on the color and pattern that will remain with them for the rest of their lives.

Behaviorisms:

Wild Sus scrofa in Europe congregate in herds, called sounders, of up to one hundred individuals, although twenty or fewer is more normal. Large sounders result from two or more dominant females joining their herds to feed in places where food is especially abundant. Sows tend to coexist peacefully at all times of year, while males eighteen months and older band together in bachelor herds or sometimes live alone during the nonbreeding months. Outsiders may be challenged by dominant animals of either sex, particularly if food is in short supply, but herd members are generally tolerant of one another.

Although wild and feral pigs are no more migratory than is necessary to find suitable habitat, they can easily cover ten miles a day. The normal gait is a trot of roughly six miles an hour, and pigs seldom walk except when feeding. At a fast run, the average adult can reach speeds in excess of twenty miles per hour.

In ancient times pigs served not just as food, but as farming animals. A plot of rough land could be tilled and made ready for planting crops just by turning a herd of pigs loose there, where the animals' rooting and pawing would loosen the soil nearly as well as a drawn plow. Early Egyptians are said to have used swine hoofprints in loose soil as planting holes for their seed, and pig dung is among the best fertilizers.

Sus scrofa's extremely acute sense of smell, which may be superior to that of a tracking dog, has also been exploited by humans to find truffles and other mushrooms. Pigs have been used experimentally for tracking people lost in the wilderness, and for finding dead bodies, although the species' temperament and lack of agility make it more difficult to work with than a dog. In medieval times pigs were sometimes trained to hunt game.

Collared Peccary

Peccaries are New World pigs, related to the warthog of Africa and the wild boar of Eurasia, but more diminutive than either of these. Peccaries have fewer teeth than true swine, and a two-chambered stomach that appears to be transitional toward the Order of ruminants (cud chewers). There are two major species: The collared peccary and the white-lipped peccary, with fourteen recognized subspecies in North and South America. All of them are known by the alternate name "javelina," which is a reference to the species' sharply pointed straight tusks that fit together tightly enough to be honed with each jaw movement.

True swine are not native to the Americas, but peccaries are found from southern North America to South America. Courtesy of Arizona Game and Fish.

Taxonomy:

Kingdom: Animalia
Phylum: Chordata
Class: Mammalia
Order: Artiodactyla
Family: Tayassuidae
Genus: Tayassu
Species: Dicotyles tajacu

Geographic Range:

Collared peccaries are found only in warmer climates, occurring from northern Argentina, throughout Central America, and northward to southern Arizona, New Mexico, and Texas.

Habitat:

In South and Central America the collared peccary inhabits tropical rainforests and lower mountain regions. In the southwestern United States and northern Mexico the preferred habitat includes rocky deserts of saguaro and mesquite. Collared peccaries are also becoming common in residential areas, where they are becoming accustomed to human garbage.

Physical Characteristics:

Mass: Thirty to sixty-five pounds.

Body: Much smaller than swine, but typically piglike, with stout barrel-shaped body on short legs. Large head with long, tapered muzzle, ending in a disc-shaped snout designed for rooting in soil. Shoulder height twenty to twenty-two inches. Body length thirty-five to forty inches. Collared peccaries have short, straight tusks that fit together tightly enough to hone one another with every jaw movement. This razor sharpness gives this species its common name: javelina (javelinlike). Javelinas have a distinct dorsal, or "precaudal," gland on the rump that secretes hormonal scents used in communication. Peccaries have poor eyesight and good hearing, which contributes to the very vocal nature of this species.

Tail: Short and inconspicuous, about three inches long, and straight, not coiled like domestic swine.

Tracks: Cloven hooves on all four feet, tracks one to one and one-half inches long. Stride is a short six to ten inches, with hind hooves usually registering in front tracks. Despite similarities to true pigs, collared peccaries comprise their own Artiodactyl suborder by having two dewclaws on the forefeet, one on the hind feet; true swine have two dewclaws on all four feet.

Scat: Typically large, almost pellet-shaped segments, much like the pellets of a deer, but larger at two to three inches long. When the peccary has been feeding on succulent plants, scat may take on a flattened disc shape similar to a cowpie. Scat may contain small bones of rodents or birds, and insect carapaces and legs.

Coloration: The peccary's coarse-haired coat is grizzled gray to nearly black with white guard hairs that give it a salt-and-pepper appearance. There is a yellowish patch on the cheeks and a collar of yellowish hair encircling the neck just ahead of the shoulders. Males and females are nearly identical in size and color.

Sign: Regularly used trails made by several animals. Feeding areas of disturbed earth, rooted up by the animals' tough snouts as they dig for roots. Chewed cactus, especially prickly pear. There will often be a strong odor of musk from the animals' urine and from a precaudal scent gland located in the middle of the back above the flanks.

Vocalizations: Grunts, squeals, growls. Peccaries are thought to be especially vocal because they possess poor long-distance vision, but it appears likely that herd

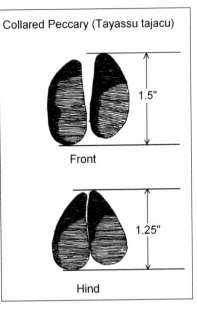

Collared Peccary (Tayassu tajacu)

1.5"

Front

1.25"

Hind

The cloven hooves of the peccary more closely resemble those of a deer than a wild boar.

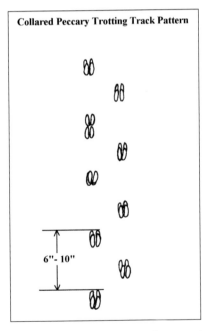

Collared Peccary Trotting Track Pattern

6"- 10"

Like wild pigs, peccaries tend to travel everywhere at a trot.

members communicate vocally to keep contact with one another in brushy terrain where visibility is limited. The alarm call is a coughing sound. Peccaries can squeal like a pig, but do so only when in mortal danger.

Lifespan: Fifteen to twenty years; up to twenty-four years in captivity.

Diet:

Collared peccaries are primarily herbivorous, with complex stomachs for digesting coarsely chewed plant material, but, like swine, they are not picky eaters. Prickly pear cactus leaves, spines and all, are a staple food in arid regions, because the succulent cacti provide both food and water, but the species also eats frogs, snakes, lizards, the eggs of ground-nesting birds, and all manner of roots, fungi, and fruits. They also eat carrion, and sometimes destroy vegetable gardens with their rooting.

Mating Habits:

Male collared peccaries reach sexual maturity at eleven months, females as early as eight months. The species does not have a set mating season, but responds to changes in climate, particularly rain, that initiate the breeding cycle. In wet weather there is a greater abundance of food, which helps to ensure that pregnant mothers are well fed, so most young are born in wet years. Conversely, in years of drought, fewer young will be born.

Peccaries are herd animals, and like other social species they have a fairly rigid hierarchy. The dominant male in a herd is the only male permitted to breed. Nonbreeding subordinate males are permitted to remain with the herd when breeding is initiated, but are not allowed to approach females in estrus. As a result, bachelor herds don't exist as they do in most herd species.

After a four-month gestation period, two to four piglets are born, with twins being the norm, and larger litters usually the result of an exceptionally well-fed mother. In contrast to most other social species that are predominantly female, the ratio between genders is approximately equal.

Pregnant females withdraw from the herd just prior to giving birth, seeking out a protected cave or other sheltered location in which to have their litters. If they don't retreat from the group they run the risk of having their young killed and possibly eaten by other herd members, especially if food is scarce. However, the risk of cannibalism is of short

Protective mothers, female javelina with young travel in small family herds called sounders. Courtesy of Arizona Game and Fish.

duration, and after one day the mother rejoins her herd, where she provides such fierce protection for her offspring that other group members leave them alone.

Peccary young are a yellowish-brown color with a black stripe down the back. They follow their mother everywhere, but are sometimes nursed by older sisters from a previous litter, the only other herd members that are allowed near the suckling piglets. Female peccaries have four nipples, but only the rear pair produce milk, forcing the mother to nurse from a standing position, and the piglets to suckle from behind her, rather than from the side as with true swine. Piglets begin to feed on vegetation within a week of being born, but are not completely weaned until they reach two to three months of age.

Behaviorisms:

Collared peccaries live in herds of five to fifteen individuals of all ages and both genders. Herds are cohesive, with members eating, sleeping, and foraging together, but there is a definite hierarchy in which a dominant male leads and the remainder are ranked primarily by size. Exceptions are the old, the terminally ill, and those seriously injured, all of which withdraw voluntarily from the group, possibly to avoid being killed and eaten by other herd members.

Although peccary herds avoid contact with groups or individuals outside their own, and will defend their territories against intruders, feeding subgroups are often formed within the same herd. These subgroups of males, females, and young sometimes form the nucleus of a new group, which breaks off from the parent herd to establish its own territory.

Peccary group territories range in size depending on herd numbers and the availability of food and other resources. Territorial boundaries are claimed by the herd leader, which rubs oily fluid from the musk gland on its rump against rocks, trees, and other prominent landmarks. Scats are also used to mark territorial boundaries, especially at trail intersections, and these will be refreshed periodically. When herd members meet one another after having been apart, they rub one another head-to-rump, each scenting the other with its own scent, thus verifying that both are members of the same group.

Herd members of either gender actively defend their territories against strangers. First comes a warning that includes laying back the ears, raising hair along the spine (hackles), and involuntary release of musk from the precaudal (rump) gland. Next comes a pawing of the ground and clacking the teeth together rapidly to make a chattering sound. If an intruder fails to withdraw, the defending peccary charges, attempting to knock the adversary off its feet, biting with its fanglike canines, and sometimes locking jaws with its opponent. Fights may be bloody, but are seldom serious for either combatant because the weaker animal will normally withdraw as soon as it becomes apparent that the other is stronger.

Collared peccaries are responsive to environmental changes, including precipitation, ambient temperatures, and length of day, and feeding behavior changes with the seasons. In winter, night foraging begins earlier in the evening and ends later in the morning as temperatures become more tolerable, and herds that would normally seek shade under which to sleep through the heat of the day in summer may forage for food at midday.

Despite their status as a game animal, especially in Arizona, collared peccaries have become habituated to residential areas, frequently making a nuisances of themselves by rooting up gardens or raiding trash cans. Their major predators—coyotes, pumas, jaguars, and bobcats—avoid human habitation, which may explain the peccary's penchant for living near people. The species is resilient and not in danger of depopulation, although about 20,000 are killed in Texas each year by sport hunters. Some subspecies living in the tropics of South America are threatened by rainforest destruction and the resultant loss of habitat.

SECTION THREE

PAWED ANIMALS

Domain: Eukarya

Kingdom: Animalia

Phylum: Chordata

Class: Mammalia

FAMILY CANIDAE

Members of the Family Canidae, or dog family, are characterized by having four feet with four toes each (discounting a dewclaw that doesn't show in tracks), each toe tipped with a non-retractable claw. A long tail is universal, as are long canine teeth designed for inflicting mortal wounds to prey. All are digitigrade, meaning they normally walk and run weight-forward, on their toes, so the heaviest impressions in a track will be from toes and claws, with heel pads printing more faintly. All are meat eaters, although all require some vegetable matter in their diets. Wild species have erect pointed ears that can swivel to precisely hone-in on sounds, and all have an acute sense of smell.

Some canids (wolves and coyotes) are social, living in families, or packs, that might comprise several generations of offspring, with a dominant "alpha" pair, who are the only members permitted to mate. Others (foxes) are solitary except for mating. Adult males universally cock a leg to urinate, usually against a stationary object, to mark territory. Females typically squat to urinate, as do males in the presence of a dominant male, but ruling females may lift one foot slightly off the ground. Urine carries numerous scents that identify an individual's territorial boundaries, gender, and sexual readiness, but also size and age. Urine posts are refreshed, often daily, and trackers should mindful that the scent posts often mark the be boundaries between two territories.

Long, strong legs, big feet for running more than 35 mph on snow and uneven terrain, sharp vision in daylight and darkness, keen hearing and sense of smell, the most massive and powerful jaws in the canid world, and a tail that never curls; all of these help to explain why tribes of old knew the gray wolf as "God's Knife."

Gray Wolf

Gray wolves are believed to be the ancestor of all domestic dog breeds, including feral breeds that include Australian dingos

(Canis lupus dingo) and New Guinea singing dogs (Canis lupus halstromi). Genetic evidence indicates that gray wolves were domesticated by humans at least twice, and possibly as many as five times.

Taxonomy:

Kingdom: Animalia
Phylum: Chordata
Class: Mammalia
Order: Carnivora
Family: Canidae
Genus: Canis
Species: Canis lupus

Geographic Range:

The gray, or timber, wolf is the largest of forty-one species of wild canids worldwide, and although all wolves in North America (except the red wolf, Canis rufus) are considered to be Canis lupus, some biologists believe there may be as many hybrids as its two regionalized subspecies.

Along with relatives of the coyote, gray wolves were once the most prevalent of wild canids, occupying most of the northern hemisphere from the Arctic through central Mexico, North Africa, and Asia. Today there are an estimated 4,500 wolves living in the lower forty-eight United States, with approximately two thousand of those living in Minnesota. Most of the balance live in Michigan, with a small planted population in Yellowstone National Park. In Canada there are an estimated 50,000 wolves, while Alaska claims about seven thousand. Both Canada and Alaska permit wolf hunting, and in 2006 gray wolves in the Eastern Management Region of Michigan, Wisconsin, and Minnesota were removed from the Endangered Species list.

In Europe, where wolves were once common, there are now only a few populations in northern Russia, Poland, Scandinavia, Spain, Portugal, and Italy. A few also survive in Japan and Mexico. The species was exterminated from Great Britain in the sixteenth century, and nearly so in Greenland during the twentieth century. Thanks to good conservation efforts, Greenland's wolf populations have regained their original strength. Wolves have shown that they can thrive in the face of advancing civilization, even expanding their range across Michigan's Straits of Mackinac in 1997 to become established at the northern tip of that state's Lower Peninsula.

Habitat:

Gray wolves are among the most adaptable mammals, able to live in a broad variety of climates and conditions. The territorial range of a pack can encompass hundreds of square miles, but there are no arbitrary ranges, because wolves range only as far as environmental factors demand. If an area provides plenty of prey and water with little competition from other large predators, a resident pack's territory may be no larger than a few square miles. In regions where a pack's food supply is migratory, as it is with caribou herds on the Arctic tundra, wolf packs may travel hundreds of miles. Studies show that road development has little effect on gray wolf migrations.

Physical Characteristics:

Mass: Sixty to 135 pounds, sometimes larger in the north; females about 10 percent smaller.

Body: Similar to a large dog, but with proportionally larger head, more massive muzzle, heavier legs. Body length (tip of nose to base of tail) forty to fifty inches. Shoulder height twenty-six to thirty-eight inches. Wolves normally move at a trot of about six mph, using only their legs for locomotion, keeping the spine very straight. This habit makes an opportunistic wolf least noticeable to prey, and is markedly different from the rocking gait of most dogs.

Gray wolf tracks.

Tail: Fourteen to twenty inches, bushy, darker on top than below, black tip. A gray wolf's tail never curls, but is always held straight down when the animal is relaxed, straight back when running, or straight up when challenged. All domestic dogs, including wolf hybrids, curl their tails.

Tracks: Largest of all canids. Front: Four to more than five inches long, discounting claws; hind: three and one-half to more than four inches. Tracks always show claws and are roughly 20 percent larger than those made by a dog of the same weight. Straddle four to six inches. Walking stride twenty-six to thirty inches. Can leap vertically more than four feet, horizontally (running) more than ten feet. Tracks are notably different than those of a coyote, and can usually be distinguished from those of a domestic dog by their larger size and physical characteristics. Like all canids, wolves have four toes on each foot, tipped with heavy, non-retractable claws, and a heel pad behind. The heel pads of the hind feet have three distinct lobes to their rear, which is typical of canines, but front heel pads show only two lobes in their tracks and leave a chevron-shaped imprint that is different from the three-lobed front tracks of a coyote, fox, and most dogs. Some dog breeds, especially Siberian and malamute huskies, also display a chevron-shaped foretrack, but these animals are smaller than gray wolves, and their tracks are much smaller.

Gray wolves have very large feet to help distribute their weight over a wider area on soft surfaces, like a snowshoe, and the front track of a ninety-pound yearling will measure at least four inches long, while a dog of the same weight will normally have a front paw that measures three and one-half inches or less. Large feet enable wolves to pursue prey over deep snows at speeds reaching thirty-five miles per hour.

Coyotes are sometimes mistaken for gray wolves, especially in winter, but a wolf is at least twice the size of its smaller cousin, with stouter legs, a broader, less-pointed muzzle, and shorter, less-pointed ears. Coyote tracks rarely exceed three inches, and where clear prints are evident the coyote's front heelpad will show three distinct lobes at its rear, where the gray wolf's front heel pad has only two, and leaves a V-shaped imprint.

Scat: Irregularly cylindrical, segmented, normally tapered at both ends. Size varies with diet and individual, but typically one and one-half to two inches in diameter, six to eight inches long. Fur and bone fragments are normally in evidence, with most fur wrapped in spiral fashion around the outside. Fresher scats are darker in color, in varying shades of brown or black, becoming gray as organic matter decomposes.

This wolf was on its toes when it made this track. The heaviest toe impression on the right side indicates that this is a right side paw print.

The scat of a gray wolf is nearly identical to that of other wild canids because all share similar diets, except that the wolf's is generally much larger in diameter and longer because the animal making it is larger. A typical scat is cylindrical and tapered at one or both ends, its outside covered in animal hair that runs longitudinally along its length. The fur wraps the outside of the scat in spiral fashion as it moves through the digestive system, surrounding bone fragments that might injure the digestive tract. More than other canids (but very similar to cougars), wolf scat will be wrapped in coarse deer hair, but may be covered with finer fur from rabbits, raccoons, and mice. An adult wolf has bite strength exceeding a half-ton per square inch, which it uses to crush large bones to obtain fat-rich marrow, and large chunks of bone in scat are a hallmark of wolf scat.

Coloration: Varied, but North American gray wolves tend to exhibit three color phases. The common gray phase is typified by combinations of white (especially guard hairs) with black, gray, red, and brown on the upper body and head. The back has a black "saddle," with most reddish fur occurring around the muzzle and ears. Belly light gray to white, with a black spot over the tail (precaudal) gland. Pups usually born black, with coats growing progressively grayer with age. Black and darkly marked wolves are typically younger than grayer wolves. Completely white coats are most often seen on Arctic subspecies in the far north.

Sign: Digging for burrowed animals is an obvious sign of gray wolves, but look for tracks, because so do bears, coyotes, and badgers. Trees that have been urinated on are territorial claims, and an indication of social status;

Gray wolf track patterns in fresh snow. Bottom to top: left front, left hind, right front, right hind.

males urinate as high up on a tree as possible to demonstrate their size. Females also urinate at scent posts, usually squatting, but sometimes raising one leg. Wolves habitually transport large prey, whole or in pieces, to a secure, often elevated, location. Gray wolves can carry a deer weighing nearly as much as themselves for half a mile, leaving traces of deer hair and hoof scrapes in the earth. Safe feeding spots may be used regularly, and littered with bones of varying ages.

Vocalizations: Like most wild animals, gray wolves are normally silent, but a social lifestyle demands communication. Howling is the wolf's most recognized sound, heard most often at dusk, when packs gather to hunt. Howling is initiated by the alpha male. Gathering howls warn other wolves (and coyotes) that this territory is claimed, and serves as a pep rally that gets pack members psyched up for the hunt. Howls are mostly monotonal, occasionally wavering, but never with the yipping or prolonged barking of coyotes and most dogs. Wolves can issue a single, deep bark when alarmed, but seem incapable of barking repeatedly.

Lifespan: About eight years in the wild; up to fifteen years in captivity.

Diet:

Gray wolves are meat eaters, but they require some vegetables to provide minerals and vitamins not provided by prey. Wolves in captivity are usually fond of green beans; those in the wild eat blueberries and other fruits, young grasses, and pine buds.

Wolves are best known as hunters of large prey, and the drill-team precision exhibited by a hunting pack is impressive, but wolves avoid prey that could injure one of their number. The prey of choice is always a weak, preferably half-dead, individual. Deer that are near death from starvation are not eaten, because toxins accumulate in muscle mass when it cannibalizes itself.

When wolf packs split up in mid-winter (when the alpha pair leaves to mate and seek out a den), they may regroup periodically to hunt larger prey, but mature pack members may strike out to find their own mates and territories. Lone wolves can rarely bring down deer, so much of their diet is mice, squirrels, rabbits, small raccoons, and other small animals.

Mating Habits:

Gray wolves mate between January and March, with those in warmer climes breeding first because spring comes to them earlier. To prevent inbreeding, only the parent, or alpha, pair will mate within a pack, which is itself a family unit. Adult offspring may leave to establish their own territories at two to four years of age, but weaker "omega" wolves may remain with the pack permanently.

As with dogs, the female's breeding cycle has four stages: anestrus, proestrus, estrus, and diestrus. The estrus stage, when the female can copulate, lasts from five to fourteen days, about half that of a domestic dog. Male wolves come into heat when females do, and, unlike dogs, their testicles, which are retracted for the rest of the year, will descend only during this period.

Two weeks prior to mating, the alpha pair separates from the rest of their pack to dig or find a den, which will always be near a source of fresh water. Typical dens consist of a body-size tunnel, roughly eighteen inches in diameter and ten feet long, excavated into the soil of hillside. This opens into a chamber about four feet high by six feet long and six feet wide, with a floor higher than the entrance tunnel to prevent flooding. Dens may also be made in small caves, so long as these afford protection from weather and predators (especially bears) that prey on pups. A den may be used year after year if left unmolested.

During the denning period adult offspring may strike out to find their own mates, while those that remain with the pack adopt younger siblings and teach them to hunt. Except for the alpha male, pack members are banned from the den site until pups are weaned, but the alpha male may regroup them for a hunt by howling. As the pregnant female becomes more vulnerable, she will spend more time in the den, and her mate will bring her food. Gestation lasts about sixty days, with most pups born between March and May, depending on how long winter lasts in that area. Average litter size is six, depending on how healthy the mother is during her pregnancy, and pups weigh about eight ounces at birth.

Newborn pups are blind and deaf. They remain in the den, completely dependent on their mother, for about eight weeks, and for their first three weeks she will stay with them constantly except for infrequent outings to drink and to expel waste. She will take at least some of her meals in the den, but its interior will be fastidiously free of refuse that might bring disease to her young. Pups grow at about three pounds per week, eating meat regurgitated by pack members returned from a hunt. Predigested meat is easier for the young pups to assimilate, and adults can carry more meat more easily in their stomachs than in their mouths.

Pups are completely weaned by nine weeks, freeing their mother to join her packmates on hunts. Pups may leave the den to play—fight with one another at this time, watched over by a "babysitter," a task usually assigned to the weakest member of the pack. By ten months of age the pups have grown to about sixty-five pounds and are old enough to hunt with the pack. Female pups reach sexual maturity at two years, and may leave the pack to find their own mates. Males typically don't reach full maturity until age three.

This photo of eastern gray wolves illustrates that a snarling, teeth-snapping wolf is not normally an indication of violence, but may be just a sign of dominance or mild displeasure in a social species that has a remarkably broad vocabulary, but only a limited number of ways to express themselves. Photo courtesy of Juan Echagarrua.

Behaviorisms:

Gray wolves are exceptionally social, with pack sizes from two recently mated animals to more than thirty in northern Canada. A typical pack is comprised of family members, usually the alpha pair and their offspring. Unrelated adults are rarely accepted into an established pack, but orphaned pups are always adopted.

A defined hierarchy exists within each pack. Alpha males are most dominant, although packs have been led by a widowed alpha female. All members are subordinate to the alphas. If the alpha male is killed, the female may leave the pack to seek out a new mate, leaving the beta, or second strongest male, to lead. It has been noted that newly paired alpha mates seeking out territories in which to establish their own pack will often travel with a third female wolf, usually a sister of the alpha female. This practice helps to ensure that a new alpha pair has the strength to take down larger prey, but also provides the alpha male with a backup mate should the original alpha female be killed. If all goes well, the secondary female will serve as a babysitter for the alphas' first litter of pups.

Members of a wolf pack virtually never fight one another, because to harm a member of the team weakens its ability to hunt. Alphas are almost never challenged from within, and the pack hierarchy is strictly followed—alphas and pups eat first, followed by betas, then subordinate pack members, and finally by the omega, or lowest ranking, wolf. Adult offspring must leave the pack to find mates, thus preventing inbreeding. Pack members are brought food if they become incapacitated, but often leave the pack voluntarily.

All gray wolf packs have an annual stationary and nomadic phase. The stationary phase occurs during spring and summer, when pups are too small to travel with their pack. The nomadic phase occurs from autumn to the late winter, when packs must travel to follow migratory or yarded deer herds. Depending on terrain and necessity, a pack may travel more than seventy-five miles in a day, most of it during the hours of darkness at a lope of about fifteen miles per hour.

Coyote

This species gets its common name from the Nahuatl Indians, who called it "coyotl." With the attrition of large carnivores, coyotes became the dominant terrestrial carnivore in North America. Coyotes have thrived in virtually every environment, and it has been argued that removing wolves from the ecosystem played a role in the coyote's rise to dominance.

Arguably the most successful and adaptable carnivore in the Americas, Canis latrans ranges from the Arctic Circle to Central America.

Taxonomy:

Kingdom: Animalia
Phylum: Chordata
Class: Mammalia
Order: Carnivora
Family: Canidae
Genus: Canis
Species: Canis latrans

Geographic Range:

Coyotes are native only to America. The species is found from Central America throughout Mexico and the lower forty-eight states, northward into central Canada and Alaska.

Habitat:

Coyotes have proved to be very adaptable over a broad range of environments and climates. They thrive in the jungles of southern Mexico, in the desert southwest of the US, and in the sometimes bitter winter cold of northern forests. The species is extraordinarily amenable to living in the vicinity of humans, having learned to recognize people as a potential food source, and in many suburban areas it has made a pest of itself by raiding garbage cans.

Physical Characteristics:

Mass: Thirty to more than sixty pounds, with the largest specimens occurring in the far north.
Body: Lanky and more slender than the gray wolf. Body length forty to more than fifty inches, height at shoulder twenty-three to twenty-six inches. Large pointed ears. Narrow tapered muzzle ending in a small black nose pad, less than one inch in diameter. Slender legs and body. The coyote is about half the size of a gray wolf and much larger than any fox. Like wolves, the eyes have a yellow iris and round pupil. The molars are structured for crushing small bones, and the canines are long and narrow.

Tail: Roughly half the body length, measuring twenty to twenty-five inches, bushy (especially in winter), and brush-shaped with a black tip. Like all canids, including dogs, there is a scent gland located on the dorsal base of the tail. Note that a coyote's tail droops normally and is held below the back when running, while a gray wolf's tail is nearly always held straight back, in line with the spine.

The track pattern of a walking coyote (bottom) contrasts with the red fox track pattern above. Coyote front track is three inches, while fox tracks are 1.5 inches. Note "mustache" at rear of the coyote's front heel pad, and that hind foot registers on top of front track.

Tracks: Compared to wolves, the feet of a coyote are relatively small for its body, averaging about two and one-half inches for the forepaws, with hind paws roughly 10 percent smaller. In northern forests there have been tracks as large as three and one-half inches recorded, but these are extraordinary. Unlike gray or red wolves, a coyote's heelpads have three lobes on all four feet, whereas wolves have only two lobes on the forefoot, three on the hind. Walking stride about fourteen inches, straddle four inches.

Scat: Similar to bobcat in size and typical composition; black to brown, growing lighter and grayer with age. Length three to more than four inches, cylindrical, segmented, about one inch in diameter. May be composed largely of blueberries in season, giving the scat a purplish color, but usually covered with fur or hair wrapped around small bones of prey animals.

Coloration: Fur varies from gray-brown to yellow-gray on the upper part, often with rust-colored patches around neck, shoulders, and flanks, and usually grizzled black on the back. The throat and belly are lightly colored, sometimes white. Forelegs, sides of the head, muzzle, and feet are reddish brown. There is one molt per year, beginning with profuse shedding in May and ending in July. Winter coats begin to grow in late August, September in more southerly ranges.

> Coyote (Canis latrans)
>
> 2.0"
> Hind
>
> 2.5"
> Front
>
> Note that the heel pads of all 4 paws have 3 lobes at the rear, but that those of the hind feet tend to print only partially, leaving a "mustache" imprint.

Sign: In winter, urine-scented tree trunks and stumps, marked by male individuals at a height of about eight inches above the ground, or about half as high up as a gray wolf. Gnawed rib ends and cartilaginous joints on deer carcasses; large leg bones will be intact, not crushed as they would be by a gray wolf.

Vocalizations: Shrill howling, barking, and yapping, almost screeching at times, especially when family members congregate at dusk or in the early morning. The scientific name, Canis latrans, is Latin for "barking dog." **Lifespan:** Eight to ten years.

Diet:

Coyotes are mostly carnivorous, but their diet includes almost any type of meat available, including lizards, snakes, grasshoppers, even fish. An average diet consists of smaller mammals like squirrels, rabbits, and especially mice. One of the best mousers in nature, coyotes may be seen standing in the middle of a field or meadow, cocking their heads and ears from one position to another as they pinpoint the location of a scurrying rodent under grass or snow. When a mouse has been located, the coyote leaps into the air, often clearing the ground with all four feet, and pounces onto its prey with the forefeet. This hunting technique is effective in winter, when rodents travel under snow through tunnels that a coyote can cave in by jumping onto the snow, thus trapping its prey. Once caught, rodents are swallowed whole.

Coyote walking track pattern in wet sand. Hind foot registers ahead of front foot, which is not uncommon.

The opportunistic coyote never passes up fresh carrion. Coyotes are often seen by sport hunters, because the little wolves have learned to associate hunters with fresh meat. In winter coyote families sometimes form a pack to hunt weakened deer, but only if smaller and more easily obtainable game like rabbits and voles are in short supply. Deer represent a large and potentially dangerous adversary to even a pack of coyotes, whose members are typically one-third the size of an adult whitetail. A sharp-hooved kick to the jaw or ribs can be fatal if it prevents a predator from eating or running fast, so deer are typically at the bottom of a coyote's list of preferred prey, and those they do hunt will always be weak, wounded, or very young.

Coyotes are fond of fruits, especially in autumn, when blueberries, wild grapes, elderberries, and other sugar—rich fruits help them to put on precious fat against the coming winter. In a good blueberry area the scat of coyotes, and all canids, will frequently be purple between the months of August and October.

Mating Habits:

Coyotes become sexually mature at twelve months, but, to prevent inbreeding, they must leave their parents' territory to find their own mates. Mated pairs are monogamous, but infrequently split up to find other mates, even after being together for several years. Male coyotes who attempt to usurp another male's mate will likely be run off by both of the mated pair.

Coyote pairs retire to a secluded denning site in January, probably using the same site year after year if it goes undisturbed. Dens are excavated, usually in the side of a ridge or rise, sometimes under the roots of a large tree, always near water, but in a place where good drainage will keep the den from flooding during the spring thaw or rains. A coyote den is a smaller version of a wolf den, consisting of a narrow tunnel about twelve inches in diameter that extends five or six feet inward, sometimes more than ten feet, terminating at a nursing chamber that measures roughly three feet high, three feet across, and about four feet long.

Mating occurs during a period between late January and March, and is usually initiated by the female, who paws at the male's flanks to indicate she's in estrous. Female coyotes are monoestrous, and remain in heat only about five days, so there is some urgency to become pregnant. Male coyotes are not fertile most of the year; like wolves, their testicles remain retracted until mating season prompts them to descend.

Actual coitus between coyote pairs occurs between February and March. Gestation is sixty days, with a litter of one to as many as nineteen pups being born in April or May. Pups weigh about seven ounces at birth. At ten days the pups will have doubled in mass and their eyes open. At three to four weeks the pups emerge from the den to play while parents protect them from birds of prey, bobcats, and bears. During this period the male brings food to his mate and offspring, feeding the young regurgitated meat, and occasionally babysitting while the mother leaves to drink or relieve herself. At thirty-five days the pups will have reached three to four pounds and are weaned.

Coyote pups grow up quickly; by six months they will have reached a weight of nearly thirty pounds, and are able to fend for themselves. By eight months the male pups will have typically left the parents to strike out on their own, while female pups may remain as part of a small pack, and to babysit future generations, for about two years.

Although the coyote is a genetically unique species, it shows a penchant for interbreeding with other canids. The red wolf (Canis rufus) is thought to be fading away as a species partly because it breeds readily with coyotes. Dogs, particularly those with pointed ears and generally coyote-like characteristics, have also mated with coyotes, producing a sometimes hard to identify "coydog." Most recently, the increased use of DNA testing in field biology has revealed that perhaps most of the gray wolves in Minnesota exhibit some coyote genes in their bloodlines.

Behaviorisms:

Coyotes are less likely than wolves to form a pack, largely because coyotes are so well equipped to catch rodents, while the larger and more powerful wolf is adapted to working in a team against larger prey animals. Coyote packs that do exist form up at dusk, with the gathering initiated by a prolonged howl from the alpha male, which is then joined by high-pitched yaps and barks from other members as they join him. Pack members may split up during the hunt, communicating the find of a meal large enough to be shared to the rest of the pack with a prolonged but broken howl that is unlike the low, monotonal howl of the gray wolf. Nightly hunts encompass areas of roughly three square miles.

Coyote territories are only as large as required to provide for their needs, but generally range from six to twelve square miles. Territories always include a source of fresh water, particularly near den sites during whelping periods, and typically include fields and meadows where mice and voles live. Territories are bounded by olfactory scent posts consisting of urine sprayed onto trees and other landmarks, and scat deposits left on regularly used trails, especially at intersections where two trails cross. Most scent marking is done by males, but alpha females may also scent claimed territories.

A very old myth that claims the coyote and the American badger (Taxidea taxus) sometimes hunt cooperatively, with the coyote using its acute nose to locate burrowing squirrels, which the badger then digs out so both predators can share the meal. The truth is more pragmatic; the coyote and badger do conspire against burrowed prey, but the badger's keen nose needs no assistance from the coyote, and the two do not share meals. The intelligent coyote has learned to position itself near the escape tunnels common to burrowing species, waiting patiently while the single-minded badger excavates inward toward its prey. The burrowed animal can wait until the badger reaches it, or it can try popping out of an escape tunnel and past the waiting coyote's lightning-fast jaws. In either instance only one of the predators is likely to be successful.

Gray Fox

Gray foxes are native to the New World, and were the reason that red foxes were brought here from Europe. When the first immigrants to America attempted to practice the nobleman's sport of fox hunting from horseback, they learned that this continent's largest native fox had an ability that was unique among canids: It could extend its semi-retractable claws and climb trees like a cat. This made for a short chase in the vast forests of the New World, so the red fox, which cannot climb trees, was imported for sporting purposes.

North America's largest native fox, the gray has never been as visible as its imported European cousin, the red fox. Courtesy National Parks Service.

Taxonomy:

Kingdom: Animalia
Phylum: Chordata
Class: Mammalia
Order: Carnivora
Family: Canidae
Genus: Urocyon
Species: Urocyon cinereoargenteus

Geographic Range:

Gray foxes are found throughout most of the southern half of North America, their range extending from southern Canada to northern Venezuela and Colombia. This species does not inhabit the more mountainous areas of the northwestern US, the Great Plains, or eastern Central America.

Habitat:

Gray foxes are most often found in deciduous forests where their unique ability to climb trees serves them in escaping predators, but may sometimes be seen in adjoining fields where they forage for grasshoppers, rodents, and berries. Unlike red foxes, gray foxes tend to avoid open agricultural areas, and are less likely to be seen by humans.

Physical Characteristics:

Mass: Seven to thirteen pounds.
Body: Typically foxlike in appearance, with long bushy tails, short legs, and a comparatively elongated body. Body length thirty-one to forty-four inches, shoulder height about fourteen inches. The head is wide, with widely spaced temporal ridges that distinguish it from other North American canids. The muzzle is narrow and tapered, ending in a small black nose pad. Ears shorter and less pointed than the red fox. Males only slightly larger than females.

Tail: Bushy, black-tipped, eight to seventeen inches long, typically shorter than that of the red fox.

Tracks: About one and one-half inches long for all four feet, hind foot slightly narrower than front. Claws semi-retractable—unique among canids—but usually show in tracks. Three lobes on heel pads of front and hind feet, but in a clear track only the outer edges of the outermost lobes will show for the hind foot.

Scat: About two and one-half inches long, one-half inch in diameter, segmented, tapered at one end, sometimes both. Often covered with fine rodent fur. Similar in shape and size to red fox scat, except that gray foxes normally eat a more vegetarian diet of berries and fruits, making their scats darker, and showing a predominance of seeds and undigested berries when these fruits are in season.

Coloration: Although most likely to be confused with a red fox, especially those in a "cross phase" of mottled red, gray, and black fur, there are identifiable differences between the coloration of red and gray foxes. The gray fox is grizzled gray and black along its back, neck, and the upper tail, much like a typical coyote. The upper head and muzzle are grizzled, with a contrasting patch of white at the tip of the muzzle, on the cheeks, and along the underbelly. Sides of the neck, legs, body, and tail are rust-colored.

Sign: Food caches buried in shallow holes and marked by loosely piled soil, sometimes with tracks evident, or wide, shallow holes left by removing cached foods. Trees that have been marked with urine at a height of about eight inches, leaving yellow stains on snow. Gray foxes are unusual among wild canids because they tend to den throughout the year, usually in natural shelters under tree roots, in rock crevices, or in hollow trees, and will often have several dens within their territories. Dens are normally much smaller than those used by coyotes, largely because coyotes prey on gray foxes, and are likely to be marked with snagged fur, bones too large to swallow, and tracks around their entrances.

Vocalizations: High-pitched barks, yaps, and growls, like a small dog. Less vocal than the red fox.

Lifespan: Eight to ten years.

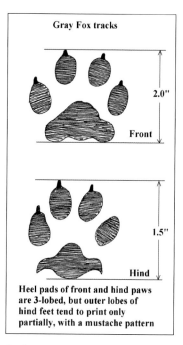

Gray Fox tracks

2.0"

Front

1.5"

Hind

Heel pads of front and hind paws are 3-lobed, but outer lobes of hind feet tend to print only partially, with a mustache pattern

Similar in size and general outline to the red fox, a gray fox's heel pads can often reveal its species in tracks.

Gray fox scat in early autumn, showing a predominance of blueberries, a vital pre-winter staple for most carnivores.

Diet:

Gray foxes have a broad and varied diet. They're good hunters, able to pounce on mice in fields or catch rabbits in brushy swamps, but the gray fox's diet has an added dimension because it can climb trees to snatch roosting birds at night, or to rob nests of their eggs. They prey on frogs, grasshoppers, and locusts, eat carrion, and catch small fish.

Gray foxes also eat vegetation, probably more than any other species of wild canid. Blueberries are a favorite when these are in season, but the gray fox can climb into the upper branches of fruiting trees, particularly wild cherries, to get fruits that are beyond reach of its non-climbing cousins.

Mating Habits:

Gray foxes mate in late winter, usually March in the northern extreme of its range, February in the warmer south. (In habitats shared by both gray and red foxes, a rule of thumb is that gray foxes mate about one month after red foxes.) Mated foxes are believed to be monogamous.

The gestation period lasts about fifty days, with up to seven pups born in a secluded woodland den in April or May. The young nurse for about three months, and during that time the father will bring his mate food, and babysit while she leaves the den to drink or relieve herself, but he takes no

The gray fox's semi-retractable claws give it a unique ability to scale trees. Courtesy Illinois Dept. of Natural Resources.

active role in parenting during the suckling stage, and doesn't enter the den.

Gray fox pups are probably the most precocious of North American canids, growing very quickly. Immediately after weaning they leave the den and begin hunting with their parents. A month later, at four months of age, the pups will have all of their permanent teeth, and weigh an average of seven pounds. At this time the pups leave their parents to fend for themselves, and the mates separate to resume a normally solitary lifestyle until the next mating season, when the pups will also be mature enough to breed. Radio telemetry data indicates that separated family members remain within their own established territories, so inbreeding is unlikely.

Behaviorisms:

Gray foxes are solitary for most of the year, and a tracker who sees one should count himself lucky. The species is reclusive and less vocal than other canids, keeping to secluded dens in shadowed woods by day and hunting at night. Their secretive behavior is explained by the fact that so many species, from large raptors and owls to coyotes to even domestic dogs consider them prey.

The gray fox is well equipped to fend for itself. Its light weight allows it to run across snow that larger carnivores would find too soft, while good night vision, excellent olfactory senses, and effective camouflage make it a formidable predator of small animals. Sharp, semi-retractable claws enable it to climb trees after sleeping squirrels, and to escape enemies that it couldn't outrun on the ground. Gray foxes have been labeled as chicken killers, but instances where they have actually been guilty are rare. Most often the culprit is a red fox (more likely a raccoon), and many times it has been simply presumed that the predator was a fox, without ever seeing it firsthand. Such leaps of logic are made more believable by adages like "a fox in the henhouse" and "sly as a fox."

Red Fox

The red fox is not native to North America, but was brought here from Europe so that noble immigrants could continue to enjoy the gentleman's sport of fox hunting with hounds from horseback. The native gray fox, with its extendable catlike claws and an ability to climb trees, was poorly suited to this pastime, so red foxes were imported to the New World. Before long the transplanted red foxes, whose adaptability to the most hostile environment is equalled only by the coyote, had escaped captivity to become firmly established as part of the American ecosystem.

A non-native that was purposely brought to America by settlers from the Old World, the red fox is a marvel of adaptability whose range extends from the Arctic Circle to Central America.

Taxonomy:

Kingdom: Animalia
Phylum: Chordata
Class: Mammalia
Order: Carnivora
Family: Canidae
Genus: Vulpes
Species: Vulpes vulpes

Geographic Range:

Red foxes have thrived in every location where they were transplanted or escaped to the wild throughout the world. Today red foxes are common throughout the continental United States, in all but the most frigid regions of Canada and Alaska—where it overlaps the range of the Arctic fox—in Australia, Japan, and across nearly all of Asia.

Habitat:

Red foxes can make their homes across an extraordinary range of habitats that includes deciduous and pine forests, Arctic tundra, open prairies, farmland, and residential districts. The species is common in suburban areas, where it preys on rats, mice, and squirrels with more efficiency than a housecat. The most preferred habitats will have a diversity of plant life, particularly fruits and berries, and especially blueberries, grapes, and cherries. Unlike the more reclusive gray fox, red foxes are frequently seen in open places.

Physical Characteristics:

Mass: Seven to fifteen pounds, with the largest individuals occurring in the far North.

Body: Slender build with a comparatively elongated body length and short legs. Body length thirty-five to forty inches; shoulder height about fifteen inches. Erect directional ears are long and pointed, with black-colored backs. The muzzle is very long and slender, tipped with a prominent black button nose. Like other wild canids, the eyes are yellow, denoting good night vision.

Tail: Very prominent and bushy. Rust-colored, thirteen to seventeen inches long, with a white tip. Like other canids, red foxes have a scent gland located on the dorsal base of the tail, identifiable by a patch of dark fur covering that area.

Tracks: Usually larger than the gray fox, but with smaller toe pads. About two and one-half inches long, hind foot slightly smaller and narrower. Four toes on each foot, with claws showing. In the North, feet are heavily furred in winter. Heel pads of all four feet are two-lobed, leaving a chevron-shaped print. The most distinguishing characteristic is a ridge that runs across the heelpad, also in a chevron shape, that prints more deeply than the rest of the pad.

Scat: Very similar to the scat of other canids, being cylindrical, segmented, and tapered at the ends, but with a predominance of berry seeds and vegetable matter when available. Often with an outer covering of rodent fur wrapped around small bones. About one-half inch in diameter by four inches long.

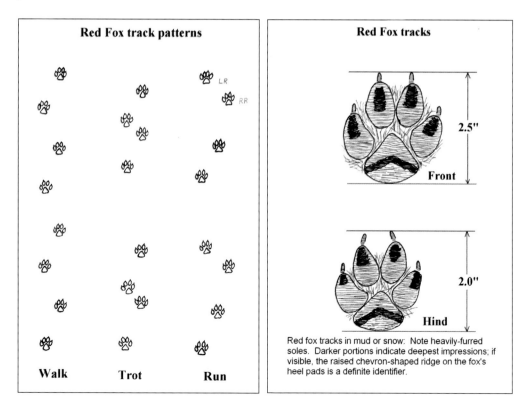

Red Fox track patterns

Walk   Trot   Run

Red Fox tracks

2.5" Front

2.0" Hind

Red fox tracks in mud or snow: Note heavily-furred soles. Darker portions indicate deepest impressions; if visible, the raised chevron-shaped ridge on the fox's heel pads is a definite identifier.

Coloration: Rust-colored to deep reddish brown on the upper parts and white to light gray on the underside. The lower part of the legs is usually black, and the tail has a white, occasionally black, tip.

A typical red fox is unlikely to be confused with any other animal, but there are two cross phases that sometimes occur, in which most or all of the fur is not red. One phase is an almost startling grizzled coat of rust-colored and black fur that covers the upper body, head, and tail. In this phase the legs are usually black and the underside reddish. There is usually a black dorsal stripe extending the length of the back, and another across the shoulders, forming the T shape that gives this color phase the name "cross fox."

Typical red fox scat, three-quarters of an inch in diameter, with segments joined together by a sheath of rodent fur, reveals a more carnivorous diet than the gray fox.

The other phase, prized by furriers, is the silver phase, in which the upper body is silver-gray with a black mask around the eyes, black ears, and dark gray to black legs. Exactly what causes these color variations is unknown, but they might stem from interbreeding with gray or Arctic foxes, or possibly from an evolutionary adaptation to different environments. Both phases are too common to be considered mutations, with cross foxes making up about 25 percent of a given population, and silver foxes about 10 percent.

Sign: Spring birthing dens excavated in the sides of hills, usually in sand, and marked by a fan of loose soil around a main entrance that may measure twelve inches across. There will always be smaller escape holes branching from the underground chamber, usually within ten feet of the main entrance. Small mounds or holes where food was cached will usually be evident near the den.

Vocalizations: Usually silent, but more vocal than the gray fox. Calls include high-pitched yapping and barking, reminiscent of a small dog. The alarm call is a single sharp, high-pitched bark, almost a short shriek.

Lifespan: Eight to ten years, sometimes longer in captivity.

Diet:

The red fox's predatory habits classify it as a carnivore, but its diet is more omnivorous. It hunts rodents, rabbits, catches small fish from shallow streams, and makes meals of grasshoppers, but when fruits and berries ripen, it may forego meat almost entirely. Blueberries are a perennial favorite, but grapes, pears, apples, and most fruits are also favored. With the high metabolic rate typical of small canids, an adult red fox may need to eat more than 10 percent of its body weight each day, and fructose is a valuable source of calories.

Red foxes are skilled hunters, especially of rodents. With a technique like that of the coyote, a fox stands motionless in a meadow, cocking its head from one side to another, and swiveling its acutely sensitive directional ears to pinpoint the location of a mouse scurrying under the grass or snow. When the fox is sure of its target, it springs high into the air, all four feet leaving the ground, and comes down hard onto the rodent with both forefeet, stunning the prey and pinning it to the earth.

Red foxes eat carrion, but with a cautious eye out for larger carnivores. One remarkable behaviorism occurs during the deer hunting seasons, when red foxes, which are bolder than most canid species, have learned to associate humans and gunshots with the rich venison liver, kidneys, and heart that most successful sport hunters leave behind.

Mating Habits:

The red fox's annual mating season relies on the arrival of warm weather, and varies by as much as four months from one region of North America to another. In the deep South, mating takes place in December and January; in the central states from January to February; in the far North between late February and April.

The annual estrous period of female, or vixen, red foxes lasts for a period of about six days. As with other canids, ovulation is spontaneous and doesn't require copulation to occur, but females signal their readiness to prospective mates through pheromonal excretions for several days prior to coming into heat. During the pre-heat period males fight almost bloodlessly to compete for breeding status. Like vixen, male red foxes have an annual cycle of fecundity in which they produce fertile sperm, being sterile the rest of the year.

Copulation lasts about fifteen minutes, punctuated by barking and yapping, mostly from the male. Females may mate with more than one male, to help ensure impregnation by the strongest genes. In a process called delayed implantation, the fertilized egg doesn't attach to the uterine wall for ten to fourteen days after mating. This delay helps to insure that the female is physically fit to bear pups; if she isn't, the fertilized egg will spontaneously abort.

On becoming pregnant the female pairs off with her strongest suitor, and they retire to a secluded location to excavate her birthing den. Although he works to make it ready, the male doesn't enter the den after its completion. Gestation lasts forty-nine to fifty-six days, with the shorter period indicating a healthy, well-fed mother, and for several days prior to giving birth the female stays close to the den, leaving only to drink and expel waste.

Between February and May, depending on latitude, the female births a litter of five to thirteen pups, or kits. Kits are born blind and weigh about three ounces, but grow quickly. By fourteen days their eyes have opened, and at five weeks pups begin playing outside of the den, running back inside at an alarm bark from their mother. Kits are weaned by ten weeks, and the father, who has provided food for his mate and regurgitated meat for his offspring, leaves to resume a solitary lifestyle. Kits remain with their mother, who teaches them to hunt and forage, until the following autumn, when pups disperse and sometimes travel more than one hundred miles before taking a mate at ten months of age.

Behaviorisms:

Able to fend for themselves, red foxes do not run in packs. The range of an adult depends on availability of resources; plenty of rodents to eat will help to keep an individual's territory small, but the nearly omnivorous red fox diet demands berries and other rich fruits, as well as a good year-round source of water. Generally, a red fox's territory will range from three to nine square miles. Fights between red foxes are rare. A good home territory will be defended against intruders, especially by females with kits. Battles are seldom more than a nip-and-chase, with the resident fox having the proverbial home advantage.

Red foxes don't den as regularly as gray foxes, although the species will have several dens throughout its territorial range, each connected to the others and to buried food caches by a series of trails that are patrolled daily or nearly so. In the case of a vixen, at least one of these will be a maternal den that's used year after year, so long as it remains undisturbed. The others, all of which have an escape exit, provide the animal with a place to duck into if chased by predators that include coyotes, wolves, and bobcats. With a running speed of about thirty miles per hour, and the ability to instantly change direction, a healthy fox has every chance of reaching safety before being overtaken by a faster carnivore.

Red foxes are known to take an occasional chicken from farmyards, but their predation is limited to small farm animals that aren't likely to fight hard.

FAMILY FELIDAE

Felidae is a family of hunters that paleontologists believe split off from other mammals during the Eocene Period, about forty million years ago. All species are endowed with acute senses of smell, hearing, and vision, and sensitive whiskers that can detect changes in air currents, possibly more. Members are well armed with very sharp retractable claws on all four of their toes, as well as a front dewclaw that can be used like a thumb to grip prey. All cats are extremely stealthy, with lightning-fast reflexes, sharply pointed canines that kill quickly with a brain-piercing bite to the base of a victim's skull, and unrivaled agility. Most prefer to hunt at night, when their well-developed night vision and binocular eyesight gives them a distinct advantage over less-well-equipped creatures. Some eat fresh carrion, but none eat animals that have been dead long enough to decay, as coyotes and bears are wont to do.

Mountain Lion

Known as cougars, pumas, painters, and cat-amounts, mountain lions are the New World's second largest felids, next to the jaguar of Mexico and South America. Historically portrayed as dangerously aggressive in novels and movies, there have been rare instances where pumas have attacked humans. Usually such aggressive cats are old ones, with bad teeth, failing health, and perhaps debilitating arthritis that keeps them from catching prey as well as they used to. Human victims are typically small-statured, alone in rural areas, and engaged in an activity that excites the feline hunting instinct the same way a wrig-

America's second-largest wild cat, the cougar is a capable hunter. Courtesy of National Park Service.

gling string triggers a compulsive instinct to attack in house cats. Breathless joggers and running children are likely victims, but skiers, snowshoers, and backpackers virtually never because they appear too large to be easy prey; the objective of any predator is not to fight, but to subdue prey with as little danger to itself as possible.

Taxonomy:

Kingdom: Animalia
Phylum: Chordata
Class: Mammalia
Order: Carnivora
Family: Felidae
Subfamily: Felinae
Genus: Puma
Species: Puma concolor

Geographic Range:

The mountain lion once had a range that spanned most of the New World from southern Argentina to northern Canada, and coast to coast across the continental United States. Because cougars posed a threat to livestock, and were a potential threat to humans, they were trapped, poisoned, and killed on sight for centuries, until only a few remained in the wildest, least traveled places. Today cougars are mostly restricted to mountainous areas in the American West, with isolated populations in South Carolina, southern Florida, Georgia, Tennessee, and Michigan.

Habitat:

Given the freedom to do so, mountain lions can utilize a broad range of habitats, from jungle and northern evergreen swamps to alpine forest and desert mountains. Deep snows, craggy rocks, and thick undergrowth are not limiting factors. Essentially, the species is capable of existing any place where they can find water, concealing cover, and enough deer-size prey to keep them well fed.

Physical Characteristics:

Mass: Seventy-five to 275 pounds.
Body: Muscular, and lithely built, very much like a domestic cat. Body length sixty to 108 inches. Legs are short, thick, and muscular, with powerful hind quarters that give the species a jacked-up appearance. The skull is broad and short, with a high arched forehead, and a broad rostrum (nasal bone). The nose pad is large and triangle-shaped. Ears are comparatively short and rounded. The mandible is powerfully constructed, the carnassial (flesh cutting) teeth are massive, and the long canines are built for making quick kills on large prey. The mountain lion's upper jaw holds one more small premolar on each side than either the bobcat or the lynx. More so than canids, the molars have a scissor-like fit, not designed for crushing bone, but for cutting hide and flesh.
Tail: One-third of the animal's total length, twenty-one to thirty-six inches long, tawny brown with a black tip.

Cougar left front track in damp sand.

Cougar right rear track in damp sand.

Tracks: Prints rounder than the elongated tracks of canids. Front prints three to more than four inches long, hind tracks about 10 percent smaller. Four large toes showing in all tracks (front dewclaw doesn't register), but normally with no claws showing because of retractable claws. Heel pads of front and hind feet have three lobes, but the front pads are blockier, less rounded. Walking stride about twenty inches, straddle eight inches.

Scat: Similar to canids; segmented, cylindrical, and tapered at one or both ends. About five inches long by one to one and one-half inches in diameter. Deer hair usually predominant, wrapped around the outer surface in spiral fashion to prevent sharp bones encased within from scratching the intestines.

Coloration: The pelage (fur coat) of a mountain lion is short and fairly coarse. Color of the upper body ranges from tan to reddish brown in summer, becoming darker and grayer during the winter months. The chest, underbelly, and mouth portion of the muzzle are white to yellowish. The backs of the ears and tip of the tail are black. A dark stripe extends downward around the

Cougar scat, about 1-inch in diameter, and a week old; note sheath of coarse deer hairs.

muzzle at either side of the pinkish nose. The eyes of adults range from bright yellow to gray-yellow.

Sign: Claw marks in trees serve as territorial scratching posts, the span and thickness of which are much broader than those of a bobcat or lynx. Scats haphazardly covered with soil will show clawmarks that are usually from the same direction in which the cat was traveling.

Vocalizations: Mountain lions purr when they're content, or when mothers are suckling kittens, and can mew like housecats. Other vocalizations include hisses, growls, and the trademark snarl. Kittens mew like domestic kittens, but have a loud chirping cry that gets their mother's attention.

Lifespan: About ten years in the wild, up to twenty years in captivity.

Diet:

Like all felids, the mountain lion prefers to kill its own food rather than eat carrion. Superbly equipped to be a hunter in terms of stealth, speed, and natural armament, a puma can take down prey larger than itself, usually leaping onto the backs of large animals and killing them with a brain-piercing bite to the base of the skull.

Best known for preying on deer-size animals, a mountain lion also eats most smaller animals, from mice and muskrats to raccoons and rabbits, and can survive well on a diet that includes no large animals. When prey is large, a puma prefers to concentrate its efforts on immature or sickly individuals that won't put up a hard fight. Annual food consumption for an adult cat is estimated at six hundred to nine hundred pounds.

Mating Habits:

Mountain lions are normally solitary, and when they come together for mating, it's a polygamous relationship, with both partners typically breeding with more than one partner. Both sexes are ready to breed at two and one-half years, but males will not mate until they've established their own territories, usually at three years. Males remain sexually fertile for up to twenty years, females to about twelve years. Mating is preceded by a courtship that allows a pair to become accustomed to one another. There is no fixed mating season, but breeding generally occurs from December to March. Males respond to pheromonal scents, yowling, and other vocalizations from females with their own eerie caterwauling, sounding much like large alley cats.

Female mountain lions mate every other year, because for the first year of their cubs' lives a mother is devoted to teaching offspring the skills of survival. The estrus period lasts for nine days, but if the female hasn't achieved pregnancy before a heat passes, she will come into estrus for another nine-day cycle.

Mating battles between males vying for a female are relatively nonviolent, consisting largely of body language, and when males do fight, the contest is largely one of physical strength, without claws or teeth. Some injuries do occur, but mountain lions harbor an instinctive revulsion against harming their own kind, and their decidedly lethal weapons are not used with the violence that they could be.

Gestation lasts from eighty-two to ninety-six days, with mothers giving birth in a secluded cave or den within the father's territory. Litter sizes range from one to six cubs with three or four being average. Newborn cubs weigh between one and two pounds, and are blind and helpless for their first ten days of life. The cubs first teeth erupt immediately thereafter, and they then begin to play. The cubs' father may bring the female gifts of food during the denning period, but takes no active role in rearing his offspring. At forty days the cubs are weaned and accompany their mother on short hunting forays.

Male cubs remain with the mother for one year before leaving to establish their own territories; female cubs may remain with her for up to two years. Male cubs that wander off together remain together for only a short time, using the strength of numbers to discourage would-be predators.

Behaviorisms:

Mountain lions are solitary animals whose lone lifestyles are interrupted only by breeding and rearing young. Territorial ranges vary from more than sixty square miles to as small as nine square miles, depending on the availability of food and water. Residents of either sex mark their territories by depositing urine or fecal materials, often at the bases of trees that serve as scratching posts.

Cougars are primarily nocturnal, with excellent night and binocular vision. Their main sense is sight, followed by sense of smell, then hearing. Pumas typically have summer and winter ranges in different locations because they follow the migratory habits of deer. The species is considered to be a threat to domestic animals, but tend to avoid human habitation.

Bobcat

The bobcat is the most dominant wild felid in North America, largely because this highly adaptable species is comfortable in a broad range of habitats. Having been hunted, trapped, or poisoned to near extinction in some places, bobcats are extremely shy of humans, and are rarely seen in places where they abound. That secretiveness may lessen as housing development continues to bring humans into bobcat habitats.

The bobcat is America's most widespread and successful wild cat. With tufted ears, a reddish spotted coat, and a pinkish nose pad, the bobcat is easy to identify.

Taxonomy:

Kingdom: Animalia
Phylum: Chordata
Class: Mammalia
Order: Carnivora
Family: Felidae
Subfamily: Felinae
Genus: Lynx
Species: Lynx rufus

Geographic Range:

Bobcats are found throughout North America from southern Mexico to southern Canada, and from the Atlantic Coast to the Pacific Coast. Population densities in the US are much higher in the forested eastern region than they are in western states. The species is rare or nonexistent in the large agricultural regions of southern Michigan, Illinois, Indiana, Ohio, and Pennsylvania.

Habitat:

Bobcats are adaptable to a wide variety of habitats, including dense forests, wet swamps, semi-arid deserts, forested mountains, and brushland. They prefer plenty of cover with trees large enough to climb for the purpose of observation or escape. The species seems well adapted to cold and snow, but isn't found in most of Canada.

Physical Characteristics:

Mass: Fourteen to more than sixty-eight pounds, with the largest specimens occurring in the northern part of the cat's range.
Body: Much like a domestic cat; lithe, well-muscled, and built for agility. Cheeks and ear tips are tuft-

ed, though not to the extent of the lynx. Body length twenty-eight to fifty inches. Shoulder height fifteen to twenty inches.

This fresh bobcat scat, about a half-inch in diameter, contains small rodent bones, wrapped in a protective outer sheath of fur.

Tail: Short, black-tipped, three to six inches long. Longer than that of the lynx, looking much like the tail of a housecat, but less than half as long.

Tracks: One to two inches long, with some as long as three and one-half inches in the far northern range. Four toes on each foot, no claws showing. All four feet approximately the same size. Stride ten to fourteen inches, straddle six to seven inches. Hind prints noted for registering precisely inside front tracks, leaving a track pattern that appears to have been made by a two-legged creature. Front of heel pad, toward toes, is concave, and distinctly different from any of the canids.

Scat: Cylindrical, segmented, tapered at one or both ends. Length two to six inches, diameter one half to one inch. Always with a predominance of rodent, rabbit, and occasionally deer, fur wrapped spiral fashion around small bones encased within. Scats are indistinguishable from those of the lynx, which has an identical diet, and easily confused with those of a coyote or fox, except that canids typically don't attempt to scratch soil over their scats. Unlike cougars, which tend to scratch soil from the direction they'll be traveling when covering scats, bobcats scratch from all directions, leaving raylike patterns of scratch marks all around the scat deposit.

Coloration: The bobcat's coat is variable, changing with the seasons. Normal summer pelage is darker brown spots against a coat of brown or reddish brown; the winter coat tends to be darker, with spots less obvious, ranging from dark brown to almost gray. In all seasons the insides of the legs, underbelly, and throat are cream colored to white, mottled with brown spots. The short tail is spotted, tipped in black.

Sign: Deep scratches in smooth barked tree trunks, about two feet above the ground, often scented with the cat's pungent urine. Soft pines seem to be the preferred scratching posts, possibly because the sticky, heavily scented sap helps to conceal the bobcat's scent while it's hunting.

Vocalizations: Much like those of a domestic cat, consisting of soft mews, purring, low growls, and childlike wailing during the breeding season.

Lifespan: Eight to ten years in the wild.

Diet:

Most of a bobcat's diet consists of prey that ranges from small rodents to rabbits to an occasional small deer. The species rarely eats carrion, preferring to kill its own food, and, like house cats, bobcats have an uncanny ability to sneak within striking distance of prey. Blue jays, grouse, and an occasional goose are caught before they can take wing and escape this wildcat's lightning-fast attack. Yearling deer may be taken by large bobcats in deep winter snows, where a strong cat can perch on a tree branch and lie in ambush. When the unsuspecting deer comes within range, the cat pounces onto its back, anchors itself there with hook-like retractable claws, and drives its long, sharp canines into the base of its victim's skull. The wound quickly kills the prey by piercing the brainstem or the spinal cord.

Officially a carnivore, the bobcat supplements its mostly meat diet with berries and some vegetable matter. Sugar calories from blueberries and other fruits are favored for putting on fat against the approaching winter, as well as for the vitamins and nutrients they contain. Grasses and sedges are also eaten, because their coarse fibers help to dislodge hairballs accumulated through grooming, and help to clear the animal's colon of undigested waste.

Mating Habits:

Bobcats in the northern range typically mate in February or March, but those in the southern range may mate throughout the summer; in especially warm areas females may produce two litters in the same year. The breeding season is initiated by the scent of a female coming into heat, which in turn attracts several suitors. After a contest that consists mostly of caterwauling, growls, and an occasional, mostly bloodless, scuffle, the strongest male mates with the receptive female, and the pair sets off to find a suitable birthing den in a rock crevice, hollow log, or under the roots of a large standing tree. No cat is well designed for digging, so dens are usually converted from existing shelters.

After a gestation period of sixty to seventy days, a small litter of two or three blind kittens, each weighing about eight ounces, is born in late April or May. After nursing for ten days, the young open their eyes and begin to move about the den. The mother stays with her kittens constantly for their first two months, leaving only to drink and to relieve herself. During this vulnerable time her mate, who doesn't enter the den, brings her food, watches over his offspring while she's out of the den, and protects the den from predators that might eat the kittens.

Bobcat kittens are weaned in June or July, and the parental pair separates, the male taking no further role in the rearing of his offspring. Kittens begin traveling and hunting with their mother, learning the finer points of catching a meal and avoiding danger, until they reach eight months of age, usually in December or January. Nearly full grown, males leave first, followed within a month by their sisters. Adolescents may disperse widely, taking up residence several miles distant, but generally travel no farther than is dictated by habitat requirements and competition from other bobcats. Emancipated kittens will likely take, or at least compete for, a mate in their first breeding season.

Behaviorisms:

Bobcats are solitary, interacting only to mate. Females are more apt to live discreetly, especially if they have kittens to protect, but males freely advertise their claim to a territory that might encompass five square miles. Partly buried scat deposits left at intersections of trails delineate territory. Pungent sprays of urine on tree trunks that may be marked by clawing do the same, but these seem most prevalent in places that are best protected.

The home range of a dominant male bobcat typically overlaps the smaller ranges of several females, giving the resident male his best chance of detecting when one of them comes into estrous. Occasionally the territorial boundaries of two males will overlap, but this seldom leads to conflict except during mating season.

Although bobcats don't normally live in dens, there are usually several refuges sited throughout an individual's range. The dens serve as a shelter for escaping foul weather that also drives most prey into hiding, or for eluding larger predators that might view a bobcat as competition, or food.

Lynx

This slightly smaller, but lankier, cousin to the bobcat is one of the most reclusive species in North America. Known variably as Lynx lynx, Felis lynx, and Lynx canadensis, this cat is supremely adapted to life in the dense timber and deep snows of the far North woods. Lynx pelts—most of them from Canada—have become increasingly valuable since restrictions were placed on the importation of cat pelts in the latter half of the twentieth century. Lynx populations have never been in danger.

The most northern and most secretive of American wild cats, the lynx is a symbol of wilderness.

Taxonomy:

Kingdom: Animalia
Phylum: Chordata
Class: Mammalia
Order: Carnivora
Family: Felidae
Subfamily: Felinae
Genus: Lynx
Species: Lynx canadensis

Geographic Range:

Never overabundant in any region, the largest populations of lynx are found throughout Canada and in the northernmost regions of Montana and Idaho. There are small populations in New England, northern Wisconsin, and in Michigan's Upper Peninsula. With a pronounced aversion to humans, warming winters, and a continually shrinking habitat, it's unlikely that lynx will ever be common.

Habitat:

Native to North America, the lynx will occasionally be seen on tundra or in rocky areas in the far North, but never far from the deep old growth forests and thick swamps that are its required habitat. The species is superbly adapted to life in deep snow, and it has a real tendency to avoid humans, so a stalker who sees one in the wild can count that day lucky.

Physical Characteristics:

Mass: Eleven to forty pounds.

Body: Long-legged with very large, furry paws adapted for silent travel in deep snow. Body length twenty-nine to forty-one inches, males about 10 percent larger than females. Pointed ears tipped with long tufts of fur, cheeks also heavily tufted, giving the appearance of thick sideburns. Height at shoulder fifteen to more than twenty inches.

Tail: Shorter than the bobcat's, two to five inches long.

Tracks: Four toes on each foot, no claws showing in tracks. Paws are extraordinarily large and well furred, especially in winter, making tracks appear even larger, but giving this fast runner a critical edge when pursuing prey over deep snow. Foreprint three to four and one-half inches long, hind prints about 10 percent smaller. Hind print with

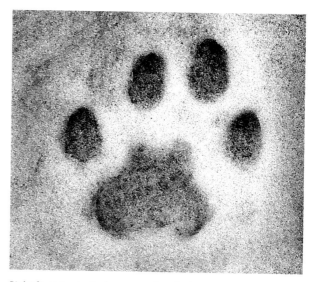

Right front track of a lynx; note that the broad foot—nature's own Snowshoe—presses evenly into the snow all around, denoting excellent balance and stealth.

three lobes at rear of heel pad, front print with three lobes on heel pad, but two outermost lobes extend more to the rear at either side, leaving a chevron-shaped impression unlike the three equal-sized lobes made by the front heel pad of a bobcat. Stride fourteen to sixteen inches, straddle five to seven inches.

Scat: Usually indistinguishable from that of a bobcat, being cylindrical, segmented, and tapered at one or both ends. Length two to six inches, diameter one-half to one inch. Scats are usually only partially buried under soil or snow, and typically have an outer covering of fine hare or rabbit fur wrapped spirally around an inner core of small bones.

Coloration: There is some variation with different individuals, but the usual lynx coat is yellow-brown in summer, becoming more gray in winter, and much longer than the fur of a bobcat. Some individuals have dark spots, but lynx generally lack the heavily spotted appearance of a bobcat. The ear tufts and tip of the tail are black, with whitish throat, underbelly, and insides of the legs. The eyes are yellow.

Sign: Scent posts on smooth-barked trees that have been clawed and sprayed with urine, partially covered scats left at the intersections of trails. Large prey that cannot be eaten entirely will often be cached by burying it beneath forest debris or snow.

Vocalizations: Normally silent except during the mating season, when males especially utter a loud shriek or scream that ends with an echoing wail that some woodsmen have described as eerie, or like the wailing of a woman.

Lifespan: Eight to ten years in the wild.

Diet:

Lynx are probably the most carnivorous felids, although they too eat grasses to help clear their digestive systems of hairballs and undigestible matter. A key species in the lynx diet is the snowshoe, or varying, hare (Lepus americanus). Being at least as proficient a hunter as its slightly larger cousin, the bobcat, the lynx is capable of catching rodents, spawning fish, and even small yearling deer given the opportunity, but survival of this species relies heavily on snowshoe hare populations. When hare populations peak and then fall in cycles, as they do about every nine and one-half years, lynx populations suffer disease and starvation one year later.

Lynx will eat carrion, but only if the meat is fresh and undecayed. Wounded deer are often eaten, especially in cold weather, but road-killed animals are often avoided because they're too close to places frequented by humans.

Mating Habits:

Like northern bobcats, and unlike southern bobcats, female lynx come into heat only once a year in March and April, and raise only one litter per year. Prior to selecting her mate, a receptive female normally has several suitors that accompany her everywhere with much wailing, caterwauling, and an occasional fight marked by hissing, spitting, and growling, but not much bloodshed. After about one week of this competition, the female enters an estrus period of just one to two days and selects a mate. After mating, the pair leaves to find a secluded birthing den in a hollow log or rock crevice.

After a gestation period of about nine weeks, females give birth in May or June to two, and sometimes as many as five, blind kittens, each weighing about seven ounces. As always, larger litter sizes are indicative of an especially healthy mother and an abundant food supply. Except for short departures to drink, urinate, or defecate, the mother lynx remains with her young constantly for their first month of life, relying on her mate to bring food and keep watch against enemies. After one month the kittens begin eating meat scraps, but continue to nurse for five months, and are weaned in October or November.

After weaning, when the kittens are grown enough to travel and learn to hunt, the male lynx leaves, and takes no part in the training of his offspring. The nearly grown young remain with their mother until January or February before setting off on their own, with males usually leaving first. Freed of her charges, the mother will come into heat again about one month later. Her female kittens reach sexual maturity at twenty months, males at thirty-three months.

Behaviorisms:

Lynx are normally solitary animals, and adults avoid one another except to mate. They are territorial, but boundaries of females may overlap peacefully, and a male's is likely to infringe on the territories of several females. Territories vary from seven to more than two hundred square miles, depending on the availability of food and resources.

Lynx are primarily nocturnal hunters, with excellent night vision and keen directional hearing. They lie in wait for hours along game trails, overlooking them from a tree branch or from behind brush, or they might stalk a prey to within a few yards, then pounce onto its back. Long canine teeth deliver a fatal bite to the base of the victim's skull, piercing its brainstem or spinal cord, enabling these cats to swiftly take down animals large enough to be dangerous to them.

While not social, hard times can prompt females with young to hunt cooperatively for hares, spreading themselves into a skirmish line and moving through brushy areas until one of them jumps prey. This hunting technique appears to be learned rather than instinctual.

Lynx shelter from foul weather in rough dens under rock ledges, in caves, under fallen trees, or in hollow logs. There are likely to be several such refuges scattered throughout an animal's territory.

FAMILY URSIDAE

The Bears (Family Ursidae)

Bears are incredible creatures. Members live in northern Europe, Asia, and India, but the three species best known are native to North America. All are large and powerfully built, ranging in weight from up to six hundred pounds for a mature black bear to more than 1,700 pounds for the massive Kodiak brown bear. All have five toes on each foot, each toe tipped with a stout, functional claw. The hind feet of all species are elongated, almost humanlike, denoting the flat-footed (plantigrade) walk of a strong, but comparatively slow-running animal that has few natural enemies.

Until the latter part of the twentieth century it was believed that bears hibernated through winter, like ground squirrels. Today we know that bears don't enter the coma-like torpor experienced by true hibernators, and sometimes leave their sleeping dens to wander during midwinter warm spells.

Most interesting to scientists are the bears' physiological attributes. Despite putting on about 25 percent of body weight in fat each year, bears suffer no arterial blockage from cholesterol. Denned bears neither defecate or urinate for months at a time, but they have a remarkable renal system that not only doesn't become toxified from a buildup of nitrogen urea, but converts this normally lethal waste product to useable amino acids, then recycles the water for use in bodily functions. If modern medicine could figure out how a bear can reprocess its own urine, the positive implications for humans suffering from kidney failure could be enormous. NASA is also keenly interested in how a bear can remain motionless in deep sleep for several months without experiencing the loss of bone mass suffered by human astronauts.

Black Bear

Smallest of North America's three native bear species, the black bear is the most abundant and adaptable. Being a natural prey of the much larger brown bear, which tops the food chain with no natural enemies, black bears are driven instinctively to avoid conflict with other large carnivores, including humans. This innate shyness means that people in the midst of black bear country seldom see one, and Ursus americanus never incurred the same wrath from people as the brown bear, whose instinct is to attack when surprised. The black bear was the original inspiration for the Teddy Bear, named after a young bear that President Theodore Roosevelt refused to kill during a hunt. Smokey the Bear, fire prevention icon of the U.S. Forestry Service, is a black bear.

Ursus americanus is unique to North America, reaching weights in excess of six hundred pounds, and able to thrive in most environments.

Taxonomy:

Kingdom: Animalia
Phylum: Chordata
Class: Mammalia
Order: Carnivora
Family: Ursidae
Subfamily: Ursinae
Genus: Ursus
Species: Ursus americanus

Geographic Range:

Native only to North America. Black bears were once common throughout North America, but by the twenty-first century, the species' range had been cut in half. Today black bears can be found south of the Arctic Circle throughout Canada and Alaska and from the Pacific Ocean to the Atlantic Coast. To the south populations are found from northern California east to the Rocky Mountains, and southward along the Rockies into central Mexico. To the east, black bears exist in healthy numbers from northern Minnesota to the north Atlantic states, with a few found along the Atlantic shoreline from New England to Florida. Black bears are not found in the Great Plains Basin of the US or Canada.

Habitat:

Black bear habitat is nearly always forested, with large trees that can be climbed to escape danger. It must always be close to fresh water, and usually contains thickets where an animal can doze the day away without being disturbed. So long as basic needs are met, suitable black bear habitat can range from hickory woods in North Carolina to the Everglades of Florida to the alpine forests of the Rockies and the fringes of prickly pear and saguaro desert.

Physical Characteristics:

Mass: Two hundred to more than six hundred pounds, males about 20 percent larger than females. The largest black bear ever recorded was a captive 880-pound boar named Tyson at Oswald's Bear Ranch in Newberry, Michigan.

Body: Stout and powerfully muscled, covered by a thick coat of fur; looks especially large in late autumn, when animals should be carrying up to 25 percent of total weight in body fat. Body length, ranges from four to more than six feet, with males only slightly (about 5 percent) larger than females. Head large and round, with short rounded muzzle and small rounded ears standing erect on either side. Although some black bears have brown fur, especially in the western part of the species' range, they're distinguished from Ursus arctos by smaller size, lack of shoulder hump, and a rounded rather than upturned nose.

Shown here is an adult black bear's walking track pattern, next to a size-10 boot for reference, showing front and hind tracks that were printed in dew-dampened sand

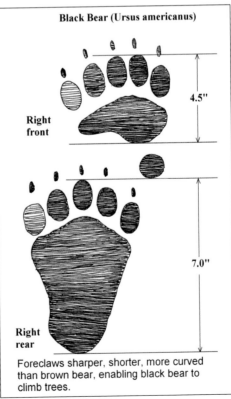

Black Bear (Ursus americanus)

Right front

4.5"

Right rear

7.0"

Foreclaws sharper, shorter, more curved than brown bear, enabling black bear to climb trees.

Tail: Short and heavily furred, three to seven inches long.

Tracks: Five forward-pointing toes on each foot, each toe tipped with a thick, curved claw that is surprisingly sharp, enabling the black bear to escape its only natural predator, the brown bear, by scaling even limbless trees. Claws always show in tracks.

Front tracks four to five inches long, six to seven inches if rear of heel pad prints, usually as a large dot, to the rear of the print. Hind prints average seven to nine inches, five inches wide at the toes, and resemble the bare footprint of a human. Like all quadrupeds, the largest, most heavily-impressed toe is to the outside, opposite our own, and clawmarks extend one inch or more ahead of each toe, sometimes printing as dots. The normal walk is a shuffling gait, with a stride of about one foot, a straddle of ten to twelve inches, and hind feet printing on top of front tracks.

Running gait is the "rocking horse" pattern common to most quadrupeds, in which forefeet are planted together as the hind feet come forward on either side. When the hind feet hit the ground, the forelegs and back are extended fully forward as the animal makes a powerful leap, coming down again on paired forefeet, and the gait repeats. Stride lengthens to three feet or more, and the pattern is paired forefeet planted side by side, bordered ahead of and to either side of the more elongated hind prints.

Scat: Massive, reflecting the size of its maker. Usually cylindrical, dark brown to black when fresh. Often smooth and unsegmented with flat, untapered ends (much like the smaller raccoon) when the diet has been mostly berries and vegetation, and insect legs or carapaces are often apparent. Deposits become more like other predators when a bear has been feeding on carrion, tapered at one or both ends, with small bones and fragments sheathed within a spiraled outer layer of fur. Length may range from segments of about two inches to scats as long as eight inches; diameter from one to more than two inches, with larger diameters indicating larger bears.

Coloration: Black bears are usually coal-black, with contrasting brown patches covering either side of the muzzle, bordering a black stripe that extends from the brow along the top of the muzzle to the nose pad. Each brow will probably be marked by a single small brown spot above each eye, much the same as some dog breeds, which denote the location of scent glands. Young bears (about two years) may have a spot of white fur on the chest.

Rich, nutritious blueberries are a much sought-after food source by many species from late summer through autumn, as this purple bear scat shows.

There are variations in the black bear's color pattern, nearly all of them seen around the Pacific coastline of North America. Black bears living west of the Great Lakes are often brown or cinnamon, and are occasionally misidentified as larger brown bears, but lack the distinctive shoulder hump. A blue-gray phase occurs near Alaska's Yukatat Peninsula, and those on Alaska's Gribble Island may be almost completely white; both of these color phases are also found in Canada's British Columbia.

Sign: Older boar (male) black bears are usually well established and can be very territorial toward intruder bears. Dominant males, usually four hundred pounds or more, use regularly refreshed scat deposits to mark the intersections of trails that bound their territories, and often employ nearby trees as scratching posts. Scratching trees are obvious to passers-by who look upward, because they consist of five usually deep gouges extending downward along the trunk from a height of up to seven feet, or as high as the individual could reach, to leave a visual record of its size. Green trees, especially poplars, aspens, and cottonwoods, are most obvious because their shredded bark hangs down in curled strips, but standing dead trees seem to be preferred for their softer, decaying texture. Manmade, usually wooden, landmarks may also be used as scratching posts, including bridges, fenceposts, and power poles.

Crushed reindeer moss lichens show the left hind and left front tracks of a bear walking toward the right of this photo. Forefoot is behind rear foot; note identifying dot shape pressed into the lichens at far left.

Sows (females) rearing cubs may be territorial, although they appear to rely more on scent than visual markers of territory. Large boars have been known to kill cubs to bring a female into heat earlier than normal, although this is less common among black bears than brown bears, so it behooves females with young cubs to be less blatantly territorial than bachelor males. Most of the obvious territorial sign a tracker finds will have been left there by males.

Other black bear sign includes large holes in meadows and knolls that were dug in pursuit of rodents. Turned-up stones and rotting logs that have been rolled over and sometimes ripped apart are a common black bear sign, especially in spring when vegetation is scarce and fat-rich grubs are abundant. In late summer, fruiting wild cherry trees are often split apart at their crotches by bears trying to reach bunches in their upper branches, a foraging practice that has not endeared them to orchard farmers.

Vocalizations: Normally silent, but can use several voices that are similar to those of brown bears. A clacking or chomping of teeth, frequently accompanied by a white froth of saliva at the corners of the mouth, indicates anxiety, and a human close enough to witness this should withdraw immediately. A loud huffing, usually issued from behind cover is another warning, and usually an invitation to leave the area. Low bawling sounds are used by mothers to communicate with cubs, while they tend to call back in louder, higher-toned bawls. Bears also bawl loudly during territorial fights, which are usually mostly bloodless wrestling matches.

Lifespan: Black bears can live as long as thirty years in captivity, but the average lifespan in the wild has been estimated at less than fifteen years.

Diet:

Black bears are the most omnivorous of North American bears. Grasses make up a large part of the diet throughout the species' range, and a black bear's digestive system can assimilate the rough fibers with nearly the same efficiency as a deer. In spring, before edible vegetation has sprouted, much of the diet consists of fat- and protein-rich larvae that have wintered inside rotting wood. They sometimes dig through the top of a large ant hill, deliberately agitating its occupants, then insert a forefoot into the mass of panicked insects; when the paw is covered by attacking ants, the bear licks them off. A typical black bear's diet varies widely from one season or region to another, and this omnivorous diet allows black bears to be the most successful species in the Ursidae family.

With a relatively slow running speed of about thirty miles per hour and a bulky body, bears are poorly designed as predators. They will appropriate deer and other kills from smaller, more skilled hunters if an opportunity presents itself, and are well equipped for excavating burrowed squirrels, but can seldom catch large prey. One exception is in late spring, when black bears prowl the thickets in search of fawns still too small to outrun them.

The territorial range of a black bear may encompass several hundred miles, but few travel more than is necessary to find food. However large a territory, it must provide sufficient nutrition to enable its owner to put on a quarter of its body weight in fat for the coming winter.

One phenomenon that trackers should be alert for in spring is the anal plug of mostly rough grasses that physically block the lower colon during the winter sleep. Prior to denning, bears eat a last meal of rough, mostly undigestible sedges, grasses, and pine needles, which mass together and form a plug in the lower intestine. The plug ensures that no excrement can foul their dens during sleep, especially not birthing dens. A tracker will find expelled anal plugs easy to identify as nearly cylindrical, two to three inches long, and comprised almost completely of long grass blades and probably pine needles, coated with a mucous-like fluid when fresh. Since bears tend to stay close to their dens for a week or so after waking, a freshly expelled anal plug is a good indication that a bear den is nearby.

Black bears have a penchant for leaving the feet of squirrel-size and larger prey, biting them free of the carcass as it feeds. The purpose is to remove the sharp climbing claws that could injure the bear's convoluted digestive system, which is unlike the straighter intestines of most carnivores.

Mating Habits:

Black bears are solitary except for the midsummer mating season. Males older than three years pair up with females older than two years in June and July for two weeks of courtship. After mating, they go their separate ways, males to mate again, if possible. By this time females with two-year-old cubs will have abandoned them, and will be ready to take another mate. Breeding sows will probably take just one mate. A sow that senses she's pregnant will ward off further advances from a male with slaps and nips.

Black bears den in November and December, just before the permanent snows fall in the northern part of their range, and only then do the fertilized eggs a sow has been carrying dormant within her womb implant to the uterine wall and begin to develop. If the sow is too unhealthy to gestate and nurse young, the eggs involuntarily abort. If a fertilized female is well fed and strong, her litter size may increase from twins, which is the norm, to as many as five cubs. Large litter sizes can be a warning sign that bears are overpopulating.

Black bear dens are less conspicuous than would seem likely for such a large animal. Den sites are in remote places where they won't be disturbed, but locations may range from excavations under the roots of a large tree to burrows in the side of a hill to large dry culverts under remote two-track roads. Den entrances are small, just large enough for an occupant to squeeze through into a larger sleeping chamber. A small space is less drafty and loses less warmth than a more voluminous area, so den sizes are typically small and efficient.

Cubs are born in January and February, after an actual gestation period of ten weeks. The naked eight-ounce cubs are usually born without waking the mother, and each of the blind newborns instinctively makes its way to a nipple. Once attached to a nipple, the cubs remain there most of the time until spring, growing rapidly. Not being a true hibernator, the mother's body temperature remains almost normal throughout winter, keeping her offspring warm while she sleeps.

When mother and newborns emerge from the den in April or May, youngsters will have grown to as much as ten times their birth size, weighing from two to five pounds. Cubs travel with their mother on her annual migration, learning the foraging, hunting, and watering places that they may continue to visit throughout their own lives. By eight months the cubs are weaned and will weigh twenty-five pounds or more. They can forage for insects and grasses, and catch an occasional rodent or frog, but are still too immature to survive on their own.

By the end of their first summer, cubs will weigh as much as seventy-five pounds, and the white blaze that most carry on their chests will have faded to black. The cubs' mother will not mate in their first year, devoting all her time and energy to teaching and protecting her young. When she dens at the onset of winter, the cubs, which have also been putting on a thick layer of fat, will den with her. When mother and cubs awaken in spring, she continues their educations until June, when the youngsters, now eighteen months old and weighing about one hundred pounds, are abandoned or chased off to allow the mother to mate again. Newly emancipated female cubs may breed in the coming season, but males wander in search of their own territories, and will not mate until they've found one, usually at age three or four. Females continue to breed every other year until about age nine, while males are normally sexually active until twelve years old.

Behaviorisms:

Black bears are most active at dawn and dusk (crepuscular), although seasonal breeding and feeding activities may alter their normal patterns. In places where they aren't disturbed by humans, bears may forage day or night.

Excepting the distractions of mating season, the overriding motivation in a bear's life is to eat, and they feed continuously from the time they awaken in spring until denning in early winter. This seemingly gluttonous behavior is an evolved response to sleeping through the lean months of winter, when plant foods are scarce or nonexistent, and only the sleek and fast predators can catch enough prey to sustain them. A bear trying to forage or hunt in deep snows would have little chance of survival, but sleeping away the winter months requires taking enough nutrition into the den with them to live until the return of warmer weather. A two-hundred-pound bear requires fifty pounds of fat to remain healthy during the winter sleep period, so the summer months must provide enough food to not only keep an individual nourished, but to make it fat.

The solitary nature of black bears can depend on the amount of food available.

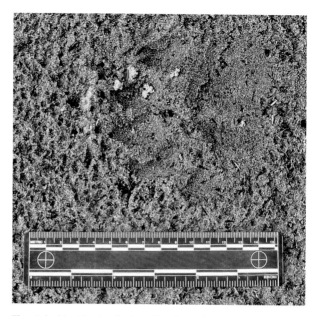

The right hind track of a bear in rain-soaked sand. Heel of the human-like foot did not print because bears and most other species walk with weight forward, on the toes.

Actually better equipped to catch fish with their sharply curved claws than grizzlies, black bears may come together along stream banks where suckers, trout, and salmon spawn. Similar congregations may be found in large tracts of ripening berries, at landfills, and at campground dumpsters. During the latter half of the twentieth century it was a favorite pastime to go to municipal dumps at dusk and watch black bears rummage through human garbage. Dump bears seem to get along well enough, so long as they respect one another's space, but humans tended to get into trouble, so today most garbage dumps are gated and locked after business hours.

Black bears have been known to kill small, easily caught livestock for food, but predations are rare. More real is the damage they inflict on corn crops, apple and cherry orchards, and bee yards. With their natural drive to feed bolstered by intelligence, curiosity, and pound-for-pound physical strength roughly twice that of a strong man, black bears can do considerable damage to crops. Ripping down grape arbors, breaking the branches of fruit trees, and trampling sweet corn crops are some of the reasons farmers have for disliking them.

Approximately 30,000 black bears are killed by sport hunters in North America each year, but the species is in no danger from overharvesting. In fact, black bear numbers may prove to be too high as housing and other development projects occupy land that was previously black bear territory. There have been numerous cases of recently emancipated cubs wandering onto the streets of rural towns, attracted there by odors emanating from restaurant dumpsters. In a few instances the trespassing animals have been shot dead, but public uproar has caused local authorities to adopt less lethal means of removing wandering bears.

Researching black bears in the field is less risky than it might sound; thirty-six humans were killed by black bears in all of the twentieth century—fewer people than are killed each year by dogs. Unlike the larger, more aggressive brown bear, which instinctively charges toward a threat, black bears are generally quick to withdraw from confrontations with humans. Mothers with small cubs are most likely to send them up a tree, then climb up after, until a potential enemy passes. Because of the species' keen sense of smell, few of the hikers detected by black bears will ever get a chance to see them.

In isolated cases, usually dominant males in excess of three hundred pounds, and especially three- or four-year-olds, have stood their ground, or even approached a human. The most unbending rule of such an encounter is never, ever run from the animal; no human can outrun a black bear, and fleeing definitely identifies you as the weaker adversary. Running away excites the bear's predatory instincts, often causing it to give chase. Standing one's ground in the face of even a large bear typically reveals that aggressive behavior, including charges that sometimes stop within a few unnerving feet, are nearly always a bluff. A person who appears unafraid and strong is less likely to be bullied by a bear.

In rare instances where Ursus americanus can legitimately be accused of attacking a person, the motivation has usually been food. Few wild animals eat human flesh, even from corpses, but an old or sickly bear that faces starvation because it can no longer make the long seasonal trek to follow its food supply might be tempted to prey on a human.

Brown Bear

Measured by weight, the brown bear is the largest land carnivore in the world, reaching twice the size of a black bear, and heavier than the taller polar bear. Brown bears have no natural enemies except other brown bears and humans, so are virtually fearless. Based on the accounts of field researchers like Doug Peacock, author of *Grizzly Years*, and anglers who share shorelines with them at places like Alaska's Denali National Park, the species is neither afraid of or hungry for humans. Like the normally harmless black bear, there have been instances where old or sickly individuals preyed on a human because it was starving, but in general brown bears regard Homo sapiens almost as they would a skunk: repulsive and annoying, but not worthy of much interest.

The massive and powerful brown bear, President Teddy Roosevelt's personal icon, resides at the top of the food chain throughout the north.

Taxonomy:

Kingdom: Animalia
Phylum: Chordata
Class: Mammalia
Order: Carnivora
Family: Ursidae
Genus: Ursus
Species: Ursus arctos horribilis (the suffix horribilis is sometimes dropped)

Geographic Range:

Brown bears once roamed most of the globe, and probably all of North America, from the Arctic Circle to Central America. But this largest of carnivores has always evoked fear in humans, the weapon-making species, and today brown bears are gone from most of their original range. An estimated population of 100,000 can still be found in northern Eurasia, with about 70,000 of those living in Russia. Isolated sightings have been reported from the Atlas Mountains of northernmost Africa, and possibly on Japan's Hokkaido Island. Brown bears were extirpated from North America's Sierra Nevada Mountains, the southern Rocky Mountains, and from northern Mexico during the twentieth century, when populations in the lower forty-eight states of the US fell from more than 100,000 animals at the turn of the century to a current low of about one thousand. Brown bear populations in Alaska and western Canada remain stable at an estimated 30,000 individuals.

Habitat:

Brown bears are at home in most habitats, but in North America the species seems partial to open areas like Arctic tundra, alpine meadows, and coastlines. Brown bears were a common sight on the Great Plains when the first European immigrants arrived. With a digestive system that can metabolize rough foliage and grasses nearly as well as deer, the bears are at home on the plains, but never far from a thicket in which to sleep. In Siberia, brown bears are more creatures of the deep forest, while European populations are confined to mountain woodlands. So long as a habitat provides vegetation, nuts, fruits, and rodents, fresh water, and a secluded place to rest, Ursus arctos can live there.

The right front paw of this brown bear dug deeply into the damp sand when the animal changed direction, while its broader hind foot left a much lighter impression.

Physical Characteristics:

Mass: Four hundred to more than 1700 pounds, males approximately 10 percent larger than females.

Body: Powerfully built, about twice the size of a typical black bear, with a distinctive large hump of muscle extending upward from the spine between the shoulders. Shoulder height four to four and one-half feet, body length six to more than seven feet, standing height ten feet or more. The head is large and broad, with small, round, furry ears at either side. Facial profile is almost concave, giving the impression of an upturned nose, unlike the rounded muzzle and profile of a black bear.

Tail: About three inches long, well-furred, and the same color as the pelage.

Tracks: Similar to those of the black bear, but larger and with longer, obvious clawmarks showing in tracks. Five toes on all four feet, with almost straight claws extending from the front toes to a length of three inches or more. Forefeet five to six inches long, discounting

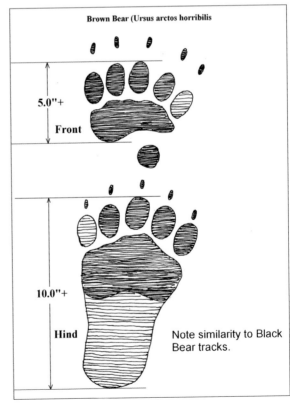

Brown Bear (Ursus arctos horribilis

5.0"+

Front

10.0"+

Hind

Note similarity to Black Bear tracks.

dot-shaped heel pad impression that may print three or four inches to the rear of the forefoot heel pad; forefoot width eight to ten inches. Hind feet ten to sixteen inches long, seven to eight inches wide, elongated, almost human shaped, and tipped with shorter claws.

Scat: Similar to a black bear's but usually larger. Generally cylindrical, often segmented, and dark brown to black when fresh, with evidence of seeds, grasses, and berries. Diameter may exceed two inches. A single scat may be broken into several segments of two to four inches in length, or when feeding on rich meats, it might be coiled and in a single

Brown and black bear scats are often identical in composition when both are feeding in the same areas, and scats of both species can be quite varied, depending on diet. This large, cowpie-like scat reflects a rich diet of mostly berries and wild cherries.

piece. Rodent and sometimes deer hair may be in evidence, wrapped spiral fashion over bones and protruding objects, much the same as scats of other predatory species.

Coloration: Fur is usually dark brown, but varies from blond to nearly black in some individuals. The common name of grizzly bear stems from the white-frosted, or grizzled, appearance of the bear's shoulders and back. The brown bear's muzzle is the same color or darker than its pelage, but never lighter colored like the black bear's muzzle.

Sign: Large excavations in hillsides and meadows where ground squirrel burrows have been dug out in search of prey. Large rocks and down logs overturned. Bathtub-size depressions in the humus of brushy thickets where a bear slept.

Vocalizations: Grunts, growls, huffing, bawling. Clacking of teeth, often accompanied by a froth of saliva around the mouth, indicates anxiety, and trackers who witness such behavior should withdraw immediately but slowly, never turning their backs to the bear.

Lifespan: Up to forty-seven years in captivity, but normally less than thirty-five years in the wild. Potential lifespan has been estimated to be as long as fifty years.

Diet:

Brown bears have a highly efficient digestive system; in spring, before many food plants have sprouted, grasses, sedges, roots, and lichens may make up the bulk of a newly awakened bear's diet. As the warm season progresses and more seasonal plants mature and bear fruit, a bear's diet and range will change to match available foods. Calorie-rich berries, nuts, and fruits are preferred, and several types of fungi are eaten, as well.

Insects in their various stages of development are eaten, too. Rotting logs and stumps are home to beetle and other larvae whose grub-like bodies are comprised mostly of fat. Spiders are eaten as they hang in their webs, and ants are gathered by sticking a big forepaw into their hill, then licking the clinging insects off with the bear's raspy tongue.

Brown bears will eat carrion when they can find or appropriate it from smaller carnivores. The seemingly instinctive hatred that exists between wolves and bears probably stems from the brown bear's practice of stealing carcasses brought down by hunting packs. Brown bears also prey on wolf pups if they can find a den of them guarded by only an Omega-wolf babysitter while the rest of the pack is away to hunt, but even a pair of wolves is usually sufficiently strong to deter a large brown bear.

Brown bears are poorly equipped for hunting prey compared to more lithe and speedy predators. In the far North, big Alaskan brown bears frequent fur seal and walrus colonies during their summer mating seasons, seeking out newborn calves, males wounded in mating battles, and individuals weak from advanced age. A brown's thirty-five miles per hour run is too slow to threaten healthy deer, but bears may follow caribou herds during their annual migrations, waiting for those most easily preyed on to reveal themselves by falling behind the herd.

Right after the bears emerge from their winter dens, but before the summer growing season has gotten underway, most of the meat eaten by a brown bear consists of small rodents and ground squirrels dug out of their burrows by its massive forepaws. With mice and vole numbers typically numbering thousands per acre, rodents can make up most of a bear's diet in spring. Marmots and ground squirrels are dug out of their dens, although many escape through exit tunnels. Like badgers, brown bears after denned prey may be shadowed by a coyote, which is itself too fast for the bear too catch. The coyote is there to exploit the bear's excavating power by guarding the prey's escape route, snapping it up if it pops out.

Salmon fishing is the best known of a brown bear's hunting skills, even becoming a tourist attraction in places like Alaska's Denali National Park. During their spring and autumn spawning seasons, mature salmon and trout migrate upstream by the thousands in the same rivers where they were born. Waiting to ambush the fish at narrows, rapids, and shallows are brown bears of all ages and sizes, which learned to come to this particular place at this time of year from their mothers. Fatty fish flesh is a critical part of the bears' diet, and the animals have learned to tolerate the presence of one another so that all can share this abundance of rich food. Sows with cubs keep their distance from adult boars, which kill, and sometimes eat, yearling cubs to induce their mother into early estrus.

Mating Habits:

Mating habits of brown bears are similar to those of the black bear. Between May and July, sexually mature sows at least three years old begin advertising their receptivity through pheromonal scents. Boars five or six years of age seek out females in heat, advertising their own availability through scat and urine deposits on trails that overlap a female's territory. After a week of courtship, the pair copulate frequently for about three days, or until the sow realizes instinctively that she is pregnant. At that point, the female tolerates no further advances from the boar, and will drive him off (to find another mate, if he can) with hard slaps and bites. Females probably take only one mate per season.

Mated sows carry fertilized eggs alive but dormant within their wombs until October or November. At this time the eggs implant to the uterine wall if the female is healthy and has put on 25 percent of her body weight in fat, or they spontaneously abort to conserve bodily resources for her own needs. Attached embryos grow rapidly; in late January to early March, two and as many as four cubs are born inside a snug excavated den. Not true hibernators, body temperatures drop only slightly and they awaken easily, but birthing mothers may sleep through delivery. Weighing about one pound at birth, blind and naked cubs make their own way to a nipple and nestle into mother's warm belly fur to nurse continuously until she awakens in April or May. At that point the cubs are fully furred, mobile, and able to travel with mother as she begins the same annual foraging trek to seasonal food sources that they will make as adults, and teach to their own offspring.

At five months, in late June to early August, cubs are weaned and begin to forage for themselves on grasses, forbs, and insects. Mothers share kills with the cubs, but they soon learn to catch rodents, frogs, and other small animals. At the end of their first summer, cubs weigh fifty pounds or more, and most smaller mammals will have become potential prey. Yearling cubs accompany their mothers to rivers to feed on spawning fish, but keep their distance from males that might kill them to drive their mother into early estrus.

Cubs den with their mothers the first winter. When she emerges the following spring they remain with her until June or July, when she abandons or drives them away to mate again. At this time, cubs weigh upwards of one hundred fifty pounds, and aren't easy prey for any carnivore. Females are less likely to breed every other year than black bears, and some sows go unmated for up to four years between litters. Emancipated cubs establish their own territories, sometimes traveling more than one hundred miles to find suitable unclaimed habitat, and continue to grow until ten years of age. Some male brown bears in Yellowstone National Park have been sexually active until twenty-five years of age.

Behaviorisms:

With no enemies except man, and no fear of anything, Ursus arctos may be active at any time of the day, but the species' foraging habits are generally crepuscular. After feeding during the cool early morning hours, warm days are spent sleeping in dense thickets. Trackers should be exceptionally careful in such close environments, and mindful that a surprised grizzly's instinct is to charge, not retreat like a black bear. Carcasses of large animals should be observed only through binoculars, never more closely than two hunndred yards, and from downwind. Brown bears camouflage carcasses too large to be eaten in a single sitting with a partial covering of leaves and debris. Carcasses are always defended, and it's a sure bet that the owner is nearby.

Territory of a male brown bear may encompass more than one thousand miles, but average is about two hundred square miles, and never more than is required to meet the bear's needs. Territories of males average seven times larger than those of females, and normally overlap the territories of several females that are potential mates. Individuals might spend several weeks in a place where fruits are plentiful, but when available foods are gone, so are the bears. The bears' omnivorous diet and nature's diversity insure that a number of food sources are available every month of its waking period.

Brown bear adults can't normally climb trees because their claws, which were sharply curved to give them that ability when they were cubs, have grown out straight and long to make them more useful as digging tools. This adaptation reflects the brown bear's open habitat, as opposed to the heavily forested environment preferred by black bears, whose sharp, curved claws permit them to climb even smooth-sided trees. This does not mean that climbing a tree is a good way to escape a brown bear, though, because there have been instances in which a bear used the branches of a large pine as ladder rungs to reach a treed human.

Brown bears have frequently been observed pushing against dead standing trees until they topple. This behavior has a real purpose, which is to stun prey animals that might be holed up inside. Once down, the trunk can be torn apart in search of grubs, ants, and sometimes the honey of a wild bee hive.

FAMILY PROCYONIDAE

Procyonids are a diverse family that includes the lesser pandas of Asia, the ringtail and coati of the southwestern US and Mexico, and the familiar raccoon. Despite the real diversity within this group, all have five toes on each foot, all are excellent climbers, all have an omnivorous diet, and all are ferocious fighters when pressed.

Raccoon

Few animals are better recognized than the raccoon, with its distinctive bandit-masked face and striped tail. Cartoons usually depict it as a thief, an allusion to its masked face, and its penchant for raiding humans. Considered prey by raptors and larger carnivores when young, an adult 'coon is ferocious when cornered, and only the largest predators are willing to tackle one. This nature is a good defense against larger predators whose objective is to kill prey with minimal effort or danger to themselves. That nature also prompts raccoons to invade residential areas to raid gardens, garbage cans, and steal an occasional chicken.

Healthy raccoons are harmless to people unless cornered. One danger they may pose is rabies, which some of them contract and die from in spring, especially when local populations are too high. Raccoons can also

Intelligent, resourceful, and equipped with hand-like forepaws that can manipulate objects nearly as well as our own, the raccoon is a real survivor, able to live in most environments. Courtesy of USFWS.

be hazardous to pets, even large dogs, and the species is known for drawing hunting dogs into deep water, where the 'coon climbs onto the dog's head, drowning it.

Taxonomy:
Kingdom: Animalia
Phylum: Chordata
Class: Mammalia
Order: Carnivora
Family: Procyonidae
Subfamily: Procyoninae
Genus: Procyon
Species: Procyon lotor

Geographic Range
Excepting the most open and arid places, raccoons are found throughout the United States from the Pacific to the Atlantic. To the North their range extends only a little north of Canada's southern border. To the south raccoons range far into Mexico, overlapping the related coati and ringtail.

Habitat:
Raccoons are intelligent and adaptable mammals, but their preferred habitat includes trees large enough to provide a good observation point or to escape predators, and will always have a source of open water. The animals are superb swimmers, able to outdistance most enemies across lakes or rivers, but they also require a water source that provides small prey like crayfish, clams, small fish, and frogs.

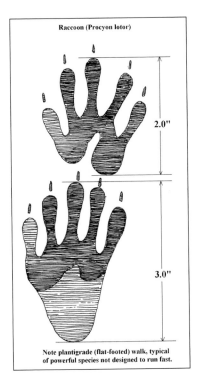

Raccoon (Procyon lotor)

2.0"

3.0"

Note plantigrade (flat-footed) walk, typical of powerful species not designed to run fast.

Physical Characteristics:
Mass: Twelve to forty-eight pounds, with an occasional individual reaching sixty pounds in the far North.
Body: Built much like a bear, stocky, muscular, and thickly furred over a layer of insulating fat. Males are generally larger than females, but the largest individuals reported have been old females. Body length twenty-three to more than thrity-eight inches, arched back eight to more than twelve inches high. Head proportionally small with short pointed muzzle tipped by a black nose. Ears erect, large, and rounded at the tips.
Tail: Striped with alternating bands of darker fur, seven to more than fourteen inches long, roughly half as long as the body.
Tracks: Easy to identify; five toes on all four feet, each toe tipped

with an elongated fingernail-like claw. Toes are long and fingerlike, with four pointing forward, and a shorter thumblike toe extending to the inside, making front paws look much like a human hand. Tips of the toes leave a bulbous impression just rearward of the claws. Forefoot length two to three inches. Hind feet are flat-soled and elongated, indicating the plantigrade walk of a slow runner that has little to fear in its daily life. The general outline is somewhat human-shaped, but has uniquely raccoon features that include four fingerlike toes pointing forward, each terminating in a bulbous tip and fingernail claw, and one shorter thumblike toe well to the rear, pointing inward. Hind foot length three to four inches.

Procyon lotor's normal gait is a shuffling walk in which soles of especially the hind feet tend to scrape the earth as they're brought forward, leaving scuff marks to the rear of the hind track. Hind prints

Track pattern of a raccoon walking in wet sand; left to right: right front, right hind, left front, left hind, right front.

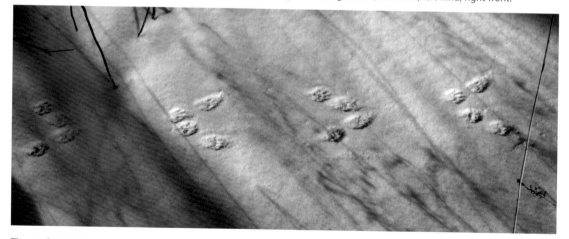

The track pattern of a raccoon running flat out over hardpack snow; note how forefeet print close together between and behind hind feet—a pattern that legendary tracker Olas J. Murie called the "rocking horse."

generally register separately and beside front tracks at a relaxed walk. The bushy tail may brush over tracks on sandy or dusty soils. Stride up to two feet between paired sets of front and hind prints. Straddle three to four inches, but can reach six inches in large animals.

At a fast run of fifteen miles per hour on flat ground, the raccoon gait changes to the almost universal "rocking horse" pattern, in which forefeet are planted side by side to act as a pivot while the hind feet are brought forward on either side. When the hind feet make contact with earth, the raccoon springs forward, forefeet extended, and the gait repeats anew. At a fast run, the distance between sets of all four tracks may exceed three feet.

Scat: Easy to identify. Cylindrical and usually unsegmented, the same diameter throughout its length. Ends usually untapered and flat. Two to three inches long by up to one-half-inch in diameter.

Coloration: The most obvious characteristics of the raccoon are its black mask around the eyes, and a bushy tail with up to ten black rings running circumferentially along its length. The pelage is grizzled, with fur color that varies from gray to reddish.

With a similar diet and digestive system, typical raccoon scats resemble miniature bear scats, with a "Tootsie Roll" shape that is unsegmented and flat on both ends, about one-half-inch in diameter.

Sign: Shells of turtle eggs that have been excavated from buried nests along sandy lakeshores. Crayfish carapaces and emptied clamshells along the banks of rivers and ponds.

Vocalizations: Most common is a chirring sound, sometimes described as cooing, made when the animal is curious or relaxed. Territorial and mating sounds include screeches, snarls, and growls.

Lifespan: Raccoons have lived up to sixteen years in captivity, but in the wild most don't make it past four years because of predation from birds of prey, land predators, and automobiles.

Diet:

Raccoons are omnivorous and opportunistic, able to subsist on a broad variety of vegetation, insects, and other small animals. Most foods are obtained along or near shorelines, where the majority of scat and sign are found. Raccoons are particularly fond of calorie-rich berries, nuts, and fruits of all types, and in many habitats, vegetation might make up most of the foods a raccoon eats. The species is fond of corn, and the normally solitary animals may descend on cornfields in force, decimating an entire field by breaking down stalks. The animals can also damage fruit trees and grape arbors by climbing them and knocking down fruit.

Poorly designed for chasing down prey, raccoons consume animal flesh whenever they can get it.

The carnivorous portion of their diets typically include more invertebrates than vertebrates. Crayfish, grasshoppers and other insects, small rodents, frogs, birds and hatchling turtles are components of the raccoons' diet—essentially, any small animal that can be taken with little effort or danger is prey. Carrion may also be eaten, but not with the same regularity as other scavengers.

Raccoons are known for their habit of washing foods at the edges of waterways, a practice alluded to by its species name, "lotor," which translates to "the washer." The purpose behind this practice is now known to be a sorting process in which the animal uses its sensitive fingerlike toes to separate inedible matter. Whereas many animals must simply swallow small prey bones and all, the raccoon can pick out the parts it doesn't want.

Mating Habits:

Raccoons become sexually mature at one year, but males will probably not breed until two years because they need to first establish their own territories. Mating season begins in late January and extends through early March, peaking in February; populations in the far South may begin mating as early as December. Males travel to females from as far as three miles, attracted to them by pheromonal scents. Mating doesn't occur immediately, but is preceded by several days of courtship, during which males den with females. Once impregnated, females reject further sexual overtures, and males go on their way, often to find another receptive female. Female raccoons are believed to take only one mate per breeding season.

After a gestation period of sixty to seventy days, females retire to a secluded leaf-lined den in a large hollow tree, under its roots, or sometimes in dry culverts, where the mother births a litter of four to eight cubs in April or May, with larger litter sizes indicating healthier females. Cubs weigh about two ounces at birth, and are blind, deaf, and almost naked (altricial). Young open their eyes at three weeks and begin to move about the den. At two months they leave the den to explore, but remain close to its entrance because cubs are prey for most carnivores and predatory birds. During this stage, the mother may move her cubs to an alternate den, carrying them one at a time by the nape of the neck. If a larger predator threatens, she will push her young up a tree, then follow them. If caught by surprise or cornered, females defend litters viciously enough to discourage most carnivores.

By three months the cubs are weaned, and begin foraging on their own for insects and small animals. The family remains together throughout the summer and following winter, but separate before the next spring mating season, when the mother will probably mate again. Males typically leave first, setting off to find their own territories, followed by female siblings who will likely take mates of their own in the coming breeding season.

Behaviorisms:

Except for mating and rearing young, raccoons are solitary. The species is generally nocturnal, but where there are no humans or, especially, dogs, they may forage along shorelines at any time. Raccoons are not true hibernators, but during periods of extreme cold or snow, they may lay up (estivate) in a den until the weather breaks, living off a normally thick layer of body fat while conserving energy. Denned raccoons are normally alone, but mothers and cubs from the previous spring den together, and courting pairs may stay together for up to one month prior to breeding.

Raccoons have highly developed tactile senses, and some researchers believe the sense of feel in their fore-paws may be several times more acute than our own. What is known is that raccoons possess the tactility needed to locate and catch snails, crayfish, and other underwater foods by feel alone. Hand-like forepaws can grasp, pull, and tear with strength sufficient to pry open clams and remove the carapaces of crayfish, or even hatchling turtles.

Raccoons (as well as skunks and badgers) are well known for digging up turtle nests, like this one, in early June, leaving small craters along shorelines that are littered with the remnants of flexible egg shells.

An ability to grasp makes the raccoon an exceptional climber. Large smooth-barked trees, like beech and sycamore, can resist the animal's relatively dull claws, but rough-barked trees like maple or white pine are easy to climb. Raccoons lack the agility to pursue prey through treetops the way a pine marten can, and generally climb only to escape enemies. On rare occasions the animals have fallen, but are able to survive long falls of thirty feet or more without serious injury.

Procyon lotor is an adept swimmer, and readily takes to the water to escape enemies. They rarely swim unless motivated by danger, however, because 'coon fur lacks the repellent oils contained in the fur of aquatic mammals, and their coat becomes heavy when saturated. If a hunting dog should pursue a raccoon into water, the raccoon is notorious for turning and climbing onto its head, holding it underwater with its own weight, and drowning the dog.

FAMILY SCIURIDAE

The family of squirrels is represented in North America by sixty-three species that include marmots, chipmunks, and tree squirrels. The family name is Latin for "shade tail," an allusion to the long bushy tail of tree squirrels, but is actually a misnomer for short-tailed ground squirrels like prairie dogs and woodchucks. Physical characteristics common to all squirrel species include having four toes on the forefeet, five toes on the hind feet. All are plantigrade, or flat-footed, with elongated hind paws that resemble human feet. All are rodents, with chisel-shaped upper and lower incisors that are adapted to gnawing and cutting vegetation, but many dine on occasional insects or small animals.

Gray Squirrel

The best-known tree squirrels among human hunters, gray squirrels have been a food staple for as long as there have been people in the New World. In Colonial America it was common to refer to any long gun that was .45 caliber or smaller as a squirrel gun, which demonstrates how important a role this tree-dwelling rodent played in the lives of pioneers. Although the eastern gray squirrel has been selected to represent larger tree squirrels here, the species has several close cousins throughout the forests of North America, and all share similar diets, mating, and behavioral traits.

One of the best survivors among tree squirrels, American Gray Squirrels transplanted in the United Kingdom have thrived to the point of becoming pests.

The same can be said of the larger fox squirrel (Sciurus niger), which shares almost exactly the same range as the gray squirrel.

Taxonomy:
Kingdom: Animalia
Phylum: Chordata
Class: Mammalia
Order: Rodentia
Suborder: Sciurognathi
Family: Sciuridae
Subfamily: Sciurinae
Genus: Sciurus
Species: Sciurus carolinensis

Geographic Range:
Sciurus carolinensis occupies the eastern half of the United States to the Mississippi River, ranging as far south as Florida and eastern Texas, and north to the southernmost edge of Canada. Introduced populations also exist in Italy, Scotland, England, and Ireland, where the squirrels have thrived to the point of becoming a serious pest.

Habitat:
Sciurus carolinensis requires a forested habitat, and will not be found in prairie, desert, or rocky places that lack tall trees in which to forage, make dens, and to escape predators. The ideal habitat includes undergrowth and ground plants, and ready access to water. Larger fox squirrels prefer a mixed habitat of conifers and hardwoods; smaller red squirrels are found in mostly coniferous forests.

Physical Characteristics:
Mass: One to one and one-half pounds.
Body: Elongated and well-furred. Short legs, rounded head with short muzzle, small round ears. Body length sixteen to twenty inches. No difference in body size between the sexes (dimorphous). Notable differences occur in skull size and fur color between gray squirrel populations in the northern and southern parts of the species' range. From north to south, skull size decreases as a regional adaptation (cline), although mandible sizes and dental arrangements remain unchanged. Also, individuals in the South tend more

Well-clawed on each of its feet, the acrobatic gray squirrel's elongated hind feet are equipped with long articulated toes for gripping, and a knobby sole to maximize surface area and traction.

toward a gray coat, while populations in the North are more often black in color and better suited to a cold climate.

Tail: Well-furred, less rounded (more flat) along its top than other tree squirrels. Length eight to ten inches, or about 50 percent of body length. Tail functions as an umbrella in rain and hot sun, and helps to keep its owner warm while sleeping in cold weather.

Tracks: Four toes on front feet, five toes hind. Tracks of front feet rounded, one to one and one-half inches long; hind feet elongated, two to two and one-half inches long. Track pattern much like a rabbit, but markedly smaller. Hind feet print ahead of forefeet, leaving a pattern like two side-by-side exclamation points (!!), indicating the hopping gait common to tree squirrels. Total length of track pattern seven to eight inches. Distance between track sets indicates gait: ten inches for a casual hopping pace, twenty-four inches at an easy bounding run, thirty-six inches or more when the animal is fleeing danger.

Scat: Pellet-shaped, dark brown to black, one-quarter-inch in diameter. Pellets often exhibit a thin "tail" of rough plant fibers on one end, indicating fibrous browse. Roughly one dozen pellets per scat deposit, depending on the size of the squirrel.

Coloration: There are two distinct color phases in S. carolinensis. Populations that live among beech trees tend to be gray, matching the smooth bark of the trees they inhabit. Those living among dark-barked trees like maples and oaks are mostly black, especially in the northern part of the range. Studies show black-furred squirrels experience 18 percent less heat loss than gray-colored squirrels in temperatures below freezing, along with a 20 percent lower metabolic rate, and a nonshivering (thermogenesis) capacity that's 11 percent higher than in grey individuals. Both color phases exhibit a grizzling of whitish guard hairs along the dorsal parts. Ears and underbelly are often lighter in color than the body. Albinism is uncommon, and doesn't

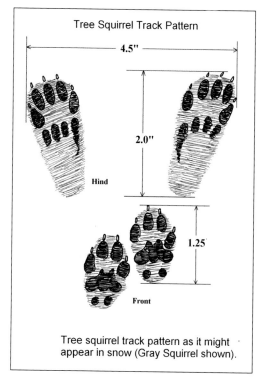

Tree Squirrel Track Pattern

Tree squirrel track pattern as it might appear in snow (Gray Squirrel shown).

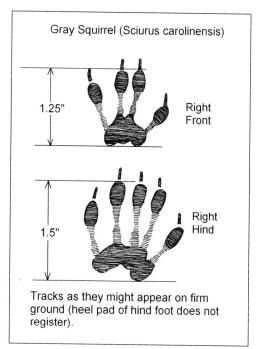

Gray Squirrel (Sciurus carolinensis)

Right Front

Right Hind

Tracks as they might appear on firm ground (heel pad of hind foot does not register).

occur at all in the colder latitudes, but albino colonies exist in southern Illinois, New Jersey, and South Carolina. Fox squirrel is larger with a reddish pelage; red squirrel is much smaller with a brown to orange coat and white underparts.

Sign: Beechnut husks, opened acorn, walnut, hickory, and other nuts. In autumn, leafy nut-bearing twigs are found beneath food trees, the cut ends showing a neatly clipped, stepped bite from the squirrel's sharp upper and lower incisors. Small patches of disturbed soil scattered atop the forest humus reveal where nuts have been buried in shallow holes for winter storage. In winter, hardpack snow will be pocked with holes, about six inches in diameter, where a squirrel burrowed diagonally downward to retrieve a buried nut, leaving a spray of darker soil atop the snow.

Vocalizations: Chirping barks are frequently heard from territorial males, especially during the autumn and spring breeding seasons. Alarm calls consist of short clucking barks that humans can usually imitate well by sucking one cheek repeatedly against the molars on one side of their mouths. The intensity of a squirrel's alarm is gauged by the frequency of the barks: a fast chattering denotes immediate danger, becoming less frequent as the source of alarm recedes.

Lifespan: Average lifespan in the wild is about twelve and one-half years, but one captive female lived to more than twenty years.

Diet:

Gray squirrels feed on nuts and seeds, with acorns, chestnuts, and other storable nuts being favored. Tree buds make up much of the diet in early spring, along with nuts that were cached in shallow holes the previous autumn. In summer the diet includes plants, grasses, and flowers. Pine and cedar nuts and buds are also eaten, and mushrooms are nibbled. Primarily vegetarian, gray and other tree squirrels are known to eat insects, tree frogs, and an occasional bird egg, with predatory habits being more common when nut crops are poor. Deer bones and antlers are gnawed to wear down the constantly growing incisors, and to get the minerals they contain. Crops like wheat, and especially corn, are favored, making the squirrels a pest species in some agricultural areas.

Legend has it that gray (and fox) squirrels remember where they buried each nut, but in fact the squirrels possess an extremely acute sense of smell that can detect cached nuts by their odors, even under a foot of snow. Not all of these buried nuts are found, however, and during good years more nuts are buried than are needed. Many unretrieved nuts take root, helping squirrels to expand their own habitats by planting trees in places where they couldn't otherwise be spread.

Mating Habits:

Gray squirrels have two mating seasons per year, one in May through June, and a second in December through February, with populations in the North breeding as much as one month later than those in the South. Males older than eleven months are drawn to pre-estrus females by the scent of sexual pheromones about a week prior to mating, and may come from as far away as half a mile. The testes of mating males become greatly enlarged prior to mating, increasing in mass from their non-breeding weight of approximately one gram to as much as seven grams at the peak of their heat.

Females may breed as young as six months, especially where population densities are low, but most mate at fifteen months, and remain fertile for about eight years. Estrus is indicated in the female by an enlarged pink vulva that makes it easier to identify the sexes, which are nearly identical during nonbreeding months. The vulva is typically swollen for just eight hours, and vaginal cavities are closed except during estrus.

Territorial battles between males are common and noisy during the mating seasons, with contenders scrapping furiously on the ground and in the trees. Embattled males are often so preoccupied that they become easy prey. In areas where populations are high or females are scarce, males have been observed actually biting off the testicles of competitors. Copulation between pairs is short, generally less than thirty seconds, after which mates go their separate ways. Males attempt to breed with as many partners as possible, but mated females breed with other partners only until they become pregnant, which they realize instinctively. After being impregnated, females form a mucous plug within their vaginal cavities that blocks further entry by sperm, and reject further sexual advances.

Gestation lasts an average forty-four days, with two to four kits born in an elevated leaf-lined nest in a hollow tree. Young are born naked (altricial) but whiskered (vibrissal), each weighing about four ounces. Newborns nurse constantly for the first seven weeks, and mothers remain with them in the nest except for short outings to eat, drink, and relieve themselves. During these brief periods the young may fall prey to raccoons, weasels, and predatory birds that can fit through the den opening, but nursing female squirrels fight viciously in defense of offspring, and predation is minimal. Still, a mother never wanders far from the nest, and her territory may shrink by half while young are suckling. Mothers may move nursing young to different nests as the situation demands. In cold months the nests are always in an enclosed den, but in warm weather young may be nursed in an open dish—shaped nest of sticks and leaves located in the crotch of a high tree limb. By ten weeks, squirrel kits have become identical to adults, and are weaned, after which the family separates and mothers provide no more maternal care. Adult size and mass are reached at nine months.

Behaviorisms:

With the exception of flying squirrels, which are nocturnal, all tree squirrels are active during daylight (diurnal), with peak activity occurring about two hours after sunrise, and two hours prior to sunset, depending on the season. They avoid activity during the heat of the day in summer, resting in loafing platforms made from sticks and leaves and located in overhead branches. Unlike maternal nests, loafing platforms are flatter and less concave because they don't contain young that might fall out. Loafing platforms are often indicative of their builder's age, with those that are more haphazardly constructed usually being made by younger, less experienced animals.

Male and female gray squirrels are identical in color and size, but the activities of an individual can provide clues to its gender. Males are most active in autumn and spring, when food, territory, and mates make them alert for competitors and more defensive. Females tend to be more active during summer and winter, when they must work to regain energy lost while rearing a litter.

Widely differing estimates have been made of how much acreage is required to support a healthy gray

squirrel, though territory size is ultimately determined by availability of resources. A single city block can be home to a half-dozen squirrels so long as sufficient food, water, and nesting sites are available, and in urban parks, where they receive regular handouts from humans, population densities may be higher. Residential areas have proved so attractive to gray squirrels that a pest-removal industry has been created in response to their invasion of attics, garages, and other places where their presence conflicts with humans. The problem is severe among transplanted populations in Great Britain, where gray squirrels are ranked second only to the Norway rat (Rattus norvegicus) in terms of property destruction.

Despite being pests in some areas, gray squirrels have a strong following among wildlife enthusiasts, and squirrel watching has become nearly as popular as bird watching. Gray and fox squirrels are also very popular with small game hunters, bringing millions of dollars in revenue to state governments and the sport hunting industry each year.

Woodchuck

Largest of the squirrel family, the woodchuck and its close relatives, the yellow-bellied marmot, hoary marmot, and Olympic marmot, are ground-dwelling burrowers that lack the bushy tail associated with tree squirrels. This species gets its common name from the Cree Indian word "woodchuck," which that tribe used to describe all marmots, but the woodchuck retained it because its burrows are most often found near forests.

Best known as the "groundhog" that emerges from hibernation each year on February 2nd to look for its shadow, the woodchuck is the most populous marmot species in North

Largest of American ground squirrels, marmots can climb trees, but prefer to live underground.

America. Because nearly all of its habits and characteristics are shared by other marmots, the information given here is generally applicable to all species.

Taxonomy:

Kingdom: Animalia
Phylum: Chordata
Class: Mammalia
Order: Rodentia
Suborder: Sciurognathi
Family: Sciuridae
Subfamily: Sciurinae
Genus: Marmota
Species: Marmota monax

Geographic Range:

The range of Marmota monax extends from the Atlantic to the Pacific across North America, extending in a line to the north from New Brunswick, across the southern shore of Hudson Bay, through the Yukon Territory, and into central Alaska. Southern boundaries extend from Virginia to Arkansas, and northwest to British Columbia. Being burrowers, they will not be found above the Arctic Circle, where permafrost prevents digging, although permafrost has been receding for more than a decade, which may cause woodchucks to expand their range northward.

Habitat:

Like all marmots, woodchucks prefer open areas where they can bask in the sun, but never far from the forests that give them their common name. Burrows excavated under the roots of large trees provide protection from digging predators like bears and wolves, while tall trees permit a quick escape for woodchucks caught by surprise on the ground. High ground with good drainage is a necessity of woodchuck habitat, especially in northern regions that experience potential flooding from snow melt in spring. Marmots require a source of drinking water nearby, but their excavated dens, which may extend underground as far as twenty-five feet and have as many as six outlets, must be in earth that remains dry year-round to a depth of at least five feet.

Physical Characteristics:

Mass: Four and one-half to fourteen pounds, with largest individuals occurring in the North. Males slightly larger and more muscular than females.

Body: Chunky and stout, with short powerful legs well adapted for digging. Body length sixteen to more than thirty-two inches. Skull broad and flat on top, flanked to either side by small roundish ears.

The woodchuck's incisors continue to grow throughout its lifespan, and if they aren't worn down properly the upper and lower mating pairs can grow past one another (malocclusion), where they may continue to grow until the jawbones are pierced and eating becomes impossible.

Marmot Track Patterns

Walking   **Running**

Tail: Three and one-half to nine inches. Well-furred but not as bushy as a tree squirrel's, about 25 percent of body length.

Tracks: Four toes on the forefeet, five toes on hind feet. The rudimentary first digit of the forepaw is covered by a flat nail; the other three digits terminate in curved claws that are useful in digging. The hind foot has five elongated and clawed digits that show clearly in most tracks. Front track about two inches long, hind track usually two and one-half inches, but three inches or more on soft ground where the entire heel prints. Straddle three and one-half to six inches; walking stride, in which hind feet print on top of or slightly ahead of front tracks, is three to four inches. In the running stride, which may be as fast as ten miles per hour, hind feet print ahead of forefeet, which print individually behind and between them; distance between track sets about fourteen inches.

Scat: Elongated and irregular in diameter, usually tapered at one or both ends, with plant fibers in evidence. Dark brown to black in color, lightening with age. Length two to more than four inches.

Marmot tracks are seldom seen in the animal's grassy or rocky environment, except at burrow entrances and escape tunnel exits, and trackers must rely on other sign to make an identification.

Coloration: Dark brown to nearly black along the dorsal region and sides, interspersed with coarser guard hairs that are banded with alternating red and yellow, tipped with white. Underbelly more pale. Head and feet much darker. Tail dark-colored, much shorter in comparison to tree squirrels. There is one molt from late May to September, which begins at the tail and progresses forward. The feet are black and plantigrade. The woodchuck's long incisors are white or nearly white, lacking the dark yellow pigmentation of other large rodents like porcupines or beavers.

Fresh marmot scat; generally teardrop-shaped, roughly one-half-inch in diameter (size varies with the size of individuals), with "tails" of undigested plant fibers.

Sign: Burrow entrances ten to fourteen inches in diameter dug into knolls and hillsides, sometimes beneath the roots of standing trees, and occasionally into and under a hole in the trunk of a standing hollow tree. The woodchuck also possesses three nipple-like anal (perineal) scent glands that secrete a musky odor, and trees, stumps, or other prominent objects around den entrances will often be scented.

Vocalizations: Woodchucks are often vocal, particularly when alarmed, which explains its nickname, "whistle-pig." The alarm cry is a single loud, shrill whistle, often preceded by a squirrel-like bark. The call used to attract mates, to warn intruders impinging on its territory, or from mothers calling young to the safety of the burrow, is a loud whistle followed by a less piercing call, and ending with a series of softer whistles that cannot be heard except at close range. Teeth grinding, chattering, and even doglike growls are common when woodchucks are cornered by a predator.

Lifespan: High attrition rate for young, but up to six years in the wild, up to ten years in captivity.

Diet:

Woodchucks are mostly herbivorous, preferring clovers, alfalfa, plantains, and grasses during the summer months, but also bark and buds of wild cherry, sumac, and other shrubs in early spring, before food plants are available. Poplar, cottonwood, and aspens are of particular importance because they provide food in the form of bark, buds, and leaves throughout the woodchuck's active time of year. Woodchucks will also eat an occasional bird egg, grasshopper, snail, or tree frog, and probably the young of most small rodents, but these minor predations appear to be opportunistic in nature. Marmots aren't known to eat carrion, but they will gnaw shed antlers and bones for the nutrients they contain.

Because the woodchuck's range and habitat encompasses most of the richest farming areas in North America, this species more than any other marmot has incurred the wrath of farmers. Lands cleared for planting provide good habitat, and crops like alfalfa, clover, wheat, and especially corn are relished

by woodchucks that can eat in excess of one and one-half pounds per animal per day, breaking down and killing plants while they feed.

In late summer, the woodchucks feed more urgently. Each animal needs to gain about 25 percent of its body weight in a layer of fat that will insulate and sustain its body through the coming winter. During this pre-denning period, a woodchuck becomes especially territorial and protective of its food resources. Trespassers, especially yearlings wandering in search of their own territories, will be decisively driven off as plants become scarcer with shortening days.

Mating Habits:

Breeding occurs in early spring, usually within two weeks after woodchucks emerge from hibernation in late March or April. Adults are normally solitary, but the territories of adult males typically overlap those of several females. This arrangement permits established males to make contact with receptive females without trespassing onto the territories of other males. When two males do compete, the battles consist of boxing matches in which both contenders stand erect on hind feet, slapping and biting one another until one withdraws.

Females are monoestrus, accepting only one mate per breeding season. Males stay in their mate's dens for about one week—the only time these normally solitary animals are social—before leaving to seek out another female. After a gestation period of approximately thirty-two days, females give birth to litters of one to nine naked and blind young, with five being the average litter size, in April or May. Newborns weigh about twenty-six grams, and measure about four inches long.

Females have four pairs of teats and nurse their young from a standing position, staying with them almost constantly for their first two weeks. At three weeks, the young begin crawling about inside the den, and at four weeks they open their eyes. By five weeks, the young woodchucks are fully active and begin exploring for short distances around the den entrance, scurrying back inside if the mother issues an alarm whistle.

Young woodchucks are weaned at six weeks, but may remain with their mother until July or August, when she forces them to disperse. Yearlings must find or excavate their own burrows after leaving their mothers, and will hibernate alone in their first winter. Females will probably mate on emerging from their dens the following spring, but competition may force young males to wait until the next spring, after they've established their own territories.

Behaviorisms:

Woodchucks are the most solitary marmot species, and both genders are generally hostile toward one another on meeting (agonistic). Battles are usually of short duration and relatively bloodless, but established adults do not tolerate trespassers. Reports of individuals sharing a den stem from observations made during the short mating period when males occupy the dens of their mates, or of nearly grown offspring denning with their mother.

Woodchucks are most often observed during the day, but may become partly nocturnal if harassed by humans. The stereotypical image of this species is an animal standing erect, forelimbs held tightly to the front of its body, as it surveys the surrounding area. Standing upright is an alert posture, but woodchucks prefer to spend their time on all fours as they feed, sunbathe, and comb their fur, never far from the den entrance. If alarmed, a woodchuck retreats into its den, turning to face outward once inside. This is a defensive position from which the marmot can bite and claw with surprising ferocity. The sharp incisors of a defensive woodchuck convince most predators to seek easier prey, but bears, badgers, and wolves can dig to the main chamber, forcing the occupant to try escape through one of up to five escape tunnels. Woodchucks are less agile than their tree squirrel cousins, but can climb trees to escape predators.

The woodchuck is a true hibernator, spending the cold winter months in a coma-like slumber within a grass-lined sleeping chamber deep inside its den. The animals enter the den to stay prior to the first permanent snowfall, usually in late November in the North, in December in the southern part of the species' range. Once inside and asleep, the marmot's body undergoes remarkable physiological changes; its body temperature falls from a normal 97° Fahrenheit to 40°, and its heart rate slows from about one hundred beats per minute to just four beats per minute. It remains in this state until warming days cause it to emerge in April, although its deep slumber appears to become lighter as spring approaches. The animals do not ritually leave their dens to see if they cast a shadow on February 2nd, but the annual Groundhog Day festival held in Punxsutawney, Pennsylvania creates enough commotion to awaken a hibernating woodchuck. This bit of American folklore, which coincides with Candlemas Day, is rooted in an Old World belief that sunny skies which allowed the European badger (meles meles) to see its shadow heralded another six weeks of winter.

FAMILY ERETHIZONTIDAE

The family of porcupines is represented throughout the world, which demonstrates the effectiveness of their common defensive weapon (the family name, "Erethizon," is Latin for "one who rises in anger"). All are slow-moving rodents that have adapted to ward off predators with hard modified hairs interspersed in the fur on their backs and tails. These "quills" are essentially sharp needles tipped with minute barbs. Because predators are almost universally evolved to kill food animals through hard physical contact using teeth and claws, these quills provide porcupines with a shield that can inflict serious, sometimes fatal injuries to attackers. A carnivore with a mouthful of embedded quills cannot eat, nor does it have the means to extract them, and most will suffer a serious infection.

Porcupine

The single species of North American porcupine has been worshiped and hated by humans, protected in some states, persecuted in others. Many a hungry woodsman, including members of the Lewis and Clark expedition, has blessed the porcupine for being the only prey he could run down and safely dispatch with a club (a hard blow across the nose usually kills it instantly). Porkies are evolved to injure predators that attack with parts of their own bodies, and they have little defense against the only carnivore able to transform its environment into an arsenal and toolbox.

With its large, low-slung bulk, the porcupine might not appear to be much of a climber, but long claws mated to articulated finger-like toes make it one of the best tree climbers in the animal world.

In some places, the porcupine's value as survival food is superseded by its importance as a pest to the timber industry. Commercially valuable pines, particularly white pines, are favored winter foods, but porcupines rarely kill mature trees (by "girdling" the smooth bark around their trunk's circumference), preferring instead to feed on younger, more tender saplings. Rural homeowners dislike that the porcupine's love for salt causes it to gnaw perspiration-soaked wooden tool handles, and even the varnish on wooden house siding. Corn crops and orchard trees may also be damaged, but female porcupines produce only one offspring per year, keeping agricultural damage low, and making populations easy to control. Evoking the most emotion are pet injuries that make even some veterinarians say they hate porcupines. In spite of prejudice toward live porcupines, Native American-made "quill boxes" crafted from bark and dyed quills fetch hundreds of dollars apiece.

Taxonomy:

Kingdom: Animalia
Phylum: Chordata
Class: Mammalia
Order: Rodentia
Suborder: Hystricognathi
Family: Erethizontidae
Genus: Erethizon
Species: Erethizon dorsatum

Geographic Range:

The common porcupine is native to boreal North America from Alaska and across Canada, south of the Arctic Circle, to Labrador. Its range covers the western half of the United States, southward from Montana through New Mexico, and into northern Mexico. In the eastern half of the US, porcupines are found only in the northernmost forested regions, covering most of New England, northern Michigan, northern Wisconsin, and northeast Minnesota.

Habitat:

Porcupines are found primarily in coniferous forests, but may spend part of the year in deciduous woods, especially in spring, when trees are budding. Preferred habitat is mixed forest of pine, deciduous hardwoods and softwoods, and a variety of ground plants, and nearly every environment will include tall trees and a source of fresh water nearby. There have been reports of porcupines frequenting riparian (riverfront) areas in mountainous regions, and even denning in rock crevices, but prefer woodlands that serve as food, shelter, and refuge from enemies.

Physical Characteristics:

Mass: Eight to forty pounds, with the largest specimens occurring in the North.
Body: Rodent-like, with humped back and short legs. Dorsal region, especially tail, covered with coarse hairs and approximately 30,000 hollow, barbed quills that can be voluntarily detached on contact, but not thrown. The longest quills occur on the rump and tail, the shortest on the neck; there are no quills

on the underbelly. Body length twenty-five to thirty-seven inches. Head small in proportion to body, and round, with short muzzle, flat face, and small round ears. Prominent yellow-orange incisors must be kept from growing past one another (malocclusion) through constant gnawing.

Tail: Large, round, and clublike, top side heavily covered with quills. Length six to twelve inches.

Tracks: Four toes on forefeet, five toes on hind feet. Toes long and articulated, each tipped with a heavy, slightly curved claw one-half to nearly one inch long.

The right front foot of this porcupine shows the unique pebbled texture of its soles.

Front track two to three inches long, including claws; hind track three to four and one-half inches long, including claws. Tracks elongated and plantigrade (flat-footed), with distinctive pebble-textured soles. At a walk, the porcupine's usual gait, hind prints register ahead of foreprints, occasionally overlapping. In snow the porky's wide, low-slung belly often drags, leaving a trough that can obscure tracks. In sand, tracks may be brushed by the heavy tail, which typically swings back and forth, leaving striated broomlike markings.

Scat: In winter, curved pellets with a sawdust-like texture, much like the muskrat's, but not connected lengthwise. Pellets are dark brown, each about one inch long, and usually distinguishable by a uniquely porcupine groove running lengthwise along the inside radius. In spring, when diet changes to succulent green plants, pellets are often shorter, with more squared ends, sometimes connected by grass fibers like a string of beads. Other forms seen from spring through autumn include formless blobs, with undigested plant fibers.

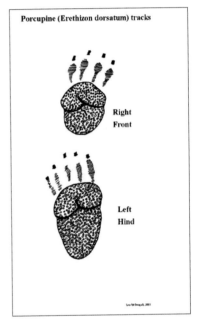

Porcupine (Erethizon dorsatum) tracks

Right
Front

Left
Hind

Coloration: Most porcupines are covered with coarse gray hairs, but some may be brown, or even black. Unquilled belly is lighter in color than back and sides. Hollow quills are black-tipped with whitish shafts.

Sign: Most obvious at all times of year are the porcupine's winter gnawing of smooth-barked pines, especially near the trees' tops, that leave irregular patches of exposed wood. In winter, there will be scattered needle-bearing twig ends lying about the snow under large pines that serve as food sources (red squirrels also nip off cone-bearing twigs from spruces and hemlocks). Den openings at the base of hollow trees generally have large accumulations of scat pellets about their entrances. Bones and antlers are gnawed to obtain the minerals in them, leaving gouges much larger than those made by smaller squirrels. Too, look for gnawings in processed lumber, especially wood that has been treated with varnish, which porcupines actually eat because of its salt content.

Vocalizations: Usually silent, even when cornered. Most vocalizations are heard during the autumn mating season, when males may grunt, squeak, and sometimes snort while in pursuit of mates.

Lifespan: Up to eight years.

Diet:

The porcupine is entirely vegetarian. In spring, before ground plants sprout, the animals climb high into poplar, aspen, and cottonwood trees to feed

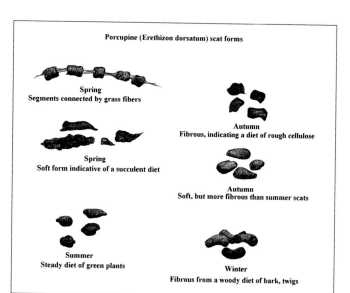

Porcupine (Erethizon dorsatum) scat forms

Spring
Segments connected by grass fibers

Spring
Soft form indicative of a succulent diet

Summer
Steady diet of green plants

Autumn
Fibrous, indicating a diet of rough cellulose

Autumn
Soft, but more fibrous than summer scats

Winter
Fibrous from a woody diet of bark, twigs

on their fleshy buds. During this brief lean period, buds of willow, staghorn sumac, beech, and many other trees and shrubs are also eaten. From spring through summer, the animals prefer green plants, including grasses and sedges, plantains, beechnuts, cresses, mustard, chickory, and dandelions. As summer progresses, the diet changes to include ripening fruits like serviceberries, blueberries, wild cherries, and apples.

When winter makes ground plants unavailable, porcupines look to trees for sustenance. They feed on bark stripped from sumac, cherries, and dogwoods, but unlike terrestrial bark-eaters, porcupines can climb into the tallest trees to reach tender bark and twig ends. Most preferred in winter are white pines, and a large tree may be occupied by a porcupine for more than a week. Preferred portions include smooth green bark, buds, and young twig ends. The animal also eats wood that has traces of salt, including sweat-soaked tool handles, plywood boats, decks, and wooden siding or shingles. In one instance, legendary tracker Olas J. Murie described how he was forced to restrain a half dozen porcupines that persisted in gnawing his canoe by looping cord around their necks and tying them to a tree until morning.

Mating Habits:

Female porcupines may mate at six months of age, but competition will likely prevent males from breeding until eighteen months. The testes of male porcupines descend into scrotal pouches between late August and early September, and development of live sperm (spermatogenesis) peaks during October. Mating occurs October through November, and during approximately sixty days of breeding, males may travel from several miles to court prospective mates. It's during this time that the normally silent porcupines are likely to be vocal, especially when several males pursue a single female into a large tree. Males are seldom violent toward one another, and never intentionally use quills on their own kind, but arboreal pursuits can be dangerous if a shoving match among the upper branches causes one

of the contestants to fall. Females are passive in the mating ritual, attracting males to themselves with pheromonal scents. Courtship is the male's domain, with squeaking and grunting, a hopping dance, treeborne contests of strength, and urinating onto the female. Females are in estrus for twelve hours, so mating is urgent and brief. If a female fails to become pregnant within that period, she will come into heat again (polyestrous) in another twenty-five to thirty days.

A longstanding jocular answer to the question of how spiny porcupines engage in sex has been "carefully," but in fact mating occurs in the same manner as other animals. When the female is ready, she voluntarily brings the quills along her back downward and holds them flat against her body, then raises her tail over her back, exposing the unquilled genitalia. The male then mounts her in conventional fashion. Once impregnated, a mucous plug forms in the female porcupine's vaginal cavity to prevent further entry by sperm, and she loses interest in mating. Her mate, who might have come from several miles distant, will set out to find another receptive female before the breeding period ends, and takes no part in the rearing of offspring.

The gestation period spans thirty weeks, which is very long for a small mammal, and probably includes a period of delayed implantation. Pregnant females give birth to a single pup (twins are rare) in April or May within a den usually located inside a standing hollow tree, sometimes in a rock crevice. Young are precocial, born fully quilled and with eyes open, but quills are soft and do not harm the mother. After being exposed to open air for about one hour, the quills harden, and the youngster becomes a smaller duplicate of its mother.

In captivity, mother porcupines have suckled their young for periods spanning several months, but youngsters in the wild are able to subsist on vegetation within two weeks. Adolescents as young as one month are capable of caring for themselves, but young porcupines accompany their mothers for five months or more, and females may mate with the same male their mothers breed with in the coming autumn. Males wander off in search of their own territories during their first summer.

Porcupine populations rise and fall in twelve-year cycles; a typical cycle consists of two years of decline, followed by a rise over the next ten years.

Behaviorisms:

Porcupines are normally solitary, and rarely show territorial aggression toward one another. In harsh weather, several adults may take shelter in the same hollow tree, cave, or culvert, with no animosity between them. When fair weather returns, the animals separate and resume their solitary lifestyles. Porcupines do not hibernate, but during the winter months pregnant females

Almost beautiful to look at, the porcupine is considered a pest by timber companies because it eats the bark of young pines in the winter.

especially seek out a birthing den. Dens are used regularly throughout the winter, and are defended against usurpers, although ownership is rarely challenged.

The entrance to a porcupine den is always marked with scat pellets, sometimes a small mountain of them if the den has been used repeatedly for several winters. When the den is inside a hollow standing tree, there will usually be a ledge inside, ten feet or more above its base, where the animal sleeps, and this platform is often partially or entirely constructed of scat pellets compressed to a hard surface under the resident's weight. Just above this elevated platform there will be a small observation hole gnawed through the tree's shell, and a sharp-eyed hiker can often spot a porcupine who lives there peering out.

On hot days, porcupines shun dens, escaping biting flies and the heat on a thick, shaded branch high up in a tree, where they can be spotted from afar as an uncharacteristic large bump. The heavily quilled tail and rump habitually point toward the tree's trunk, the direction from which predators must approach. This strategy will frustrate most bobcats, raccoons, and most climbing carnivores, but the fisher is able to clamber past the porcupine along the underside of the branch to emerge in front of it, thereby gaining access to its unprotected head.

Porcupines prefer to forage at night. Just before sunset they emerge from dens and sleeping trees to forage for ground plants. Only the most hungry or inexperienced predators chance tackling a foraging porky, but if one does, the porcupine points its tail end toward the enemy, turning as the predator circles to keep its most potent armament in position for a spiny slap. Given an opportunity, the porcupine will escape by climbing a tree.

FAMILY LEPORIDAE

This is the family of rabbits and hares. Rabbits (genus Sylvilagus) are sometimes confused with hares (genus Lepus), but there are physical traits that distinguish the two: Rabbits are generally smaller, with shorter ears and shorter legs. Being the faster runner, hares are more prone to open areas, while rabbits prefer brushy habitats where they can hide. Hares give birth to fully furred young in relatively open places, while rabbit newborns are born naked in a sheltering burrow or nest, and require a more prolonged period of maternal care. Both are prolific breeders, with reproductive rates adapted to offset heavy predation from numerous carnivores.

Rabbits and hares are not rodents, but members of the Order Lagomorpha, a group that also includes the diminutive pikas. A defining difference between lagomorphs and rodents is a second smaller and shorter pair of incisor teeth directly behind the chisel-like upper incisors, which serve as a cutting board of sorts. This dental arrangement gives the animals a very sharp scissor-like cutting action when nibbling fibrous sedges, permitting them to chop tough cellulose into fine pieces that digest more easily. Lagomorphs are also remarkable in that males carry their scrotum ahead of the penis, instead of behind it, a characteristic seen only in marsupials.

Worldwide, there are eighty species of lagomorphs, categorized in thirteen genera, grouped into two families, Leporidae (rabbits and hares) and Ochotonidae (pikas). Native populations of lagomorphs are found on all continents except Antarctica, southern South America, and Australia (introduced populations of lagomorphs in Australia have thrived to the point of becoming pests).

Snowshoe Hare

Also known as the "varying hare" because individuals in the species' northern range grow a white coat in winter, the snowshoe hare gets its common name from oversized hind feet that give it exceptional flotation on deep snow and muddy marshes. One of the smallest hares, the snowshoe "jackrabbit" is a vital prey species for many carnivores, especially the lynx and bobcat.

Taxonomy:

Kingdom: Animalia
Phylum: Chordata
Class: Mammalia
Order: Lagomorpha
Family: Leporidae
Genus: Lepus
Species: Lepus americanus

The snowshoe hare hasn't quite changed into its white winter coat, which has been grizzled brown all summer. Courtesy USFWS.

Geographic Range:

Snowshoe hares inhabit the northern United States from New England through New York, Michigan, northern Wisconsin, northern Minnesota, and northern North Dakota. To the south, their range extends only along mountain ranges that are snow-covered in winter, to northern California along the Cascade Mountains, to Colorado along the Rockies, through West Virginia and Virginia along the Allegheny and Appalachian mountain ranges. To the north, snowshoes inhabit nearly all of Canada and Alaska south of the Arctic Circle. Perhaps notably, the snowshoe hare's northern range meets, but rarely overlaps, that of the Arctic hare (Lepus arcticus), with a precise demarcation line between the ranges of either species.

Habitat:

Unlike rabbits, which tend toward thickets and prefer to hide from danger, snowshoe hares prefer more open areas where they can rely on powerful hindquarters and large feet to speed them out of reach of predators at speeds exceeding twenty-five miles per hour. Secluded bogs, marshes, and swamps are preferred during daylight hours, but at night the hares venture out to feed in more open areas, like fields and meadows, shorelines, and roadside ditches.

Physical Characteristics:

Mass: Two to more than four pounds, less than half the weight of larger hare species; about the same weight as an eastern cottontail rabbit, with which the snowshoe shares much of its range.
Body: Rabbitlike, humped back, long powerful hind legs, disproportionately long and wide hind feet.

Body length fifteen to twenty-one inches. Head round, muzzle blunt, large eyes at either side of the head. Ears shorter than those of most other hares to lessen loss of heat from them in cold temperatures, ear length roughly three inches. Males (bucks) are slightly smaller than females (does)—unusual among mammals, but typical among leporids.
Tail: Dark gray to black on top, whitish below, one to two inches long.
Tracks: Four toes on front and hind feet. Forefeet comparatively round, one and one-half to two inches

long; hind feet very large, with widely spread toes, three to four and one-half inches long. In winter, tracks may be obscured by a heavy coat of fur on the underside. Hind feet print ahead of forefeet at a casual hop, leaving a track pattern that looks like paired exclamation points (!!), similar to those of a tree squirrel, but several times larger. At a relaxed hop, a set of all four tracks measures ten to sixteen inches. Distance between track sets may be more than fifteen feet, with longer leaps denoting a faster pace.

Scat: Typical of all rabbits and hares; generally marble- or egg-shaped, occasionally acorn-shaped, with spherical forms usually indicating a diet of drier, less succulent vegetation. Diameter about one-half inch. Color usually dark brown when fresh, becoming lighter colored and more sawdust-like with age. Scat pellets are generally found in groups of a half-dozen or more.

Note that rabbits and hares possess a digestive process known as "cecal fermentation," in which rough cellulose is eaten, excreted (pooped out) as spheres, then re-eaten for final digestion. During the first stage, pellets are green, and a tracker who finds them can presume that his appearance frightened off their owner.

Coloration: Brown in summer, becoming grizzled with age, with a darker dorsal line, and longer fur than the cottontail. Underside whitish, face brown, ear tips black; often has a white patch on top of the head. In snow country the animal's coat turns entirely white except for black tips on the ears. Snowshoes in Washington and Oregon normally don't exhibit this photoperiodic color change, remaining brown all year, and in New York's Adirondack Mountains there is a population that remains black (melanistic) all year.

Snowshoe hares are known for their seasonal molts. The winter molt usually begins in November as a patchy, mottled coat of white spots that become larger until the animal is completely white, a process that takes about seventy days

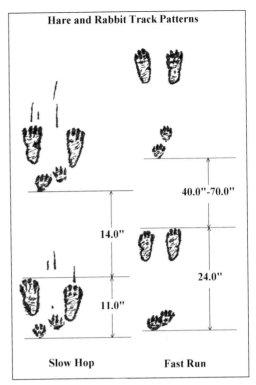

Hare and Rabbit Track Patterns

40.0"-70.0"

14.0"

24.0"

11.0"

Slow Hop   Fast Run

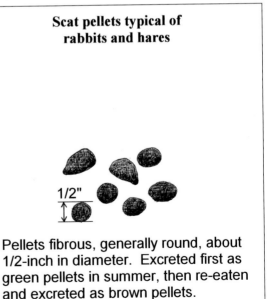

Scat pellets typical of rabbits and hares

1/2"

Pellets fibrous, generally round, about 1/2-inch in diameter. Excreted first as green pellets in summer, then re-eaten and excreted as brown pellets.

to complete. Snowshoes possess two separate sets of hair follicles, one that grows only white hairs, the other growing the brown and gray hairs of the summer coat. Color phases are regulated by daylight, not temperature, which during warm winters can result in white hares that contrast starkly against bare ground.

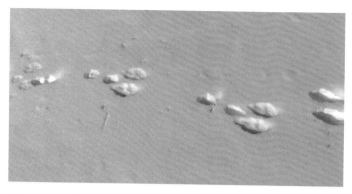

This snowshoe hare was traveling at an easy hop; note that forefeet print close together and behind more widely-spaced hind feet.

Sign: Typical of rabbits and hares; stripped, barkless shrubs like sumac, dogwood, and willow during the winter months. Neatly clipped grasses and ground plants in summer. Trails are often regularly used and well-packed; trails in snow may be packed to a depth of more than one foot, permitting high speed travel in troughs too narrow for predators to use.

Vocalizations: Normally silent. Mothers purr to young while nursing. Newborns whimper and whine. The alarm cry is a prolonged squeal, normally heard only when a hare has fallen into the grip of a predator. In all cases the calls of a hare are lower-toned than those of a rabbit. When battling over territory, two hares may growl and hiss. Also heard occasionally is the thumping of a hind foot being pounded repeatedly against the earth, especially when the animal suspects danger, but can't locate its source—a ploy to entice a predator into revealing itself.

Lifespan: Few snowshoe hares die of old age, but become prey to a host of predators as soon as their reflexes slow, and most don't reach adulthood. Average lifespan three or four years.

Diet:

The snowshoe hare's diet is more broadly varied than other leporids, but normally vegetarian. The animals graze on grasses, vetches, asters, jewelweed, wild strawberry, pussy-toes, dandelions, clovers, and horsetails, as well as the buds of aspen, poplar, birch, and willow. In winter, snowshoe hares forage on buds, twigs, bark, and the tips of evergreen twigs. If plant foods are scarce, they may eat carrion, and have been known to raid traps baited for carnivores to get meat.

This snowshoe hare demonstrates the effectiveness of its white winter coat. (Photo courtesy National Park Service).

A notable trait among leporids is their need to eat the same food twice. Much of the hare's diet is tough cellulose, and because most of its digestive processes are contained in the lower gut, foods must be eaten, excreted, then re-eaten to extract all the nutrients from them. This process, called "cecal fermentation," permits the animals to quickly ingest food plants where feeding may be hazardous, then retire to a safer location where they can be completely digested at leisure.

Despite being considered food by so many carnivorous species, snowshoes are among nature's best survivors, a fact that can be seen in the lack of fat on their bodies. With a broad diet that encompasses almost every type of vegetation, as well as carrion when times get hard, the hares have little need to carry food reserves on their bodies. But they do need to maintain a body that is lean and muscular to escape fleet-footed predators like the coyote. Mountain men of old, for whom hares and rabbits were a staple winter food, often found themselves suffering from "rabbit starvation" by winter's end. Fat malnutrition can occur—as it did with the Lewis and Clark expedition—when fats are lacking in the diet, even when plenty of other foods are available.

Mating Habits:

Breeding season of the snowshoe hare runs throughout the summer months, beginning in March, when the males' testicles descend, and extending through August, when the testicles retract and become dormant. Males pursue females by their pheromonal scents, frequently congregating around receptive does in groups.

Mating contests between breeding males resemble boxing matches in which both contenders rise on hind legs and bat at the muzzles of one another with sharp-clawed forefeet. If one of the combatants is knocked onto its back, the powerful, clawed hind feet are used to kick and scratch against an adversary's underside. Despite the apparent ferocity of these battles, they usually end quickly, when the weaker animal withdraws, and are seldom seriously injurious to either party.

Snowshoe does are polyestrus, coming into heat whenever they aren't pregnant throughout the summer months, and both genders engage in sex with different mates almost indiscriminately (polygynandrous). This seemingly lascivious behavior helps to insure that these prolific breeders have a strong, widely varied gene pool.

Gestation takes thirty-five days, with litters of two to eight fully furred precocial young being birthed in a makeshift nest atop the ground, but sometimes in the recently abandoned burrow of a fox or coyote. The young hares are able to run within two hours of birth, and begin feeding on vegetation their first day. Mothers nurse their litters for about thirty days, but will probably become pregnant again before they're weaned. Adult does may birth as many as four litters per summer, and newborn females may begin mating almost as soon as they've been weaned. The species' rapid reproduction rate makes it resistant to heavy predation from the many meat-eaters that hunt it, and makes it unlikely that snowshoe hares will become a concern for conservationists.

Behaviorisms:

Snowshoe hares are solitary animals, but population densities are often high enough to force them to live together. Under ideal conditions, an adult's territory may encompass as much as eighteen acres, but when populations peak, the amount of land an individual can claim may shrink to a fraction of that size. Actual population densities may range from one to as many as 10,000 individuals per square mile, with numbers typically increasing steadily for a period of about nine years, then drastically falling off in the following year. Direct causes for this sudden decline, which appears to be a normal phenomenon with this species, include sudden epidemics of pneumonia, severe fungal infections, salmonella, and tularemia. The root cause of these plaguelike illnesses is most likely malnutrition brought on by depletion of food resources. A secondary effect of the snowshoe's cyclic decline is a sudden decline in populations of the lynx, which relies heavily on hares in its own diet, about one year later.

Notably, the greatest fluctuations in snowshoe hare populations occur in northwestern Canada, and the least in Colorado's Rocky Mountains. Explanations for this phenomenon include greater diversity among predator and prey species in the warmer regions, while colder climates tend to less varied, with relationships between hunter and hunted being more critically symbiotic.

Lepus americanus isn't classified as nocturnal, but the hares do show a reluctance to be active in sunlight. In clear summer weather the animals are most likely to feed and breed during the hours between dusk and dawn, but may also be seen foraging at midday when skies are overcast or rainy.

Snowshoes have very good directional hearing, a keen sense of smell, and large protruding eyeballs positioned at either side of the head that permit them to detect approaching danger, but they tend to freeze, relying on their natural camouflage, unless a predator's body language reveals that it has seen them. When a hare does run from danger, it zig zags through underbrush at high speed, changing direction instantly to make itself hard to follow visually, as well as physically. Like whitetailed deer and rabbits, the hares rely on a maze of trails, each scented with frequent scat deposits, to confuse the most acute sense of smell. Although they can run fast and erratically enough to outmaneuver predators in thick cover, snowshoe hares must escape quickly, because they tire after a few hundred yards, while their main enemies can maintain top running speed for a mile or more. When it begins to slow from exhaustion, a hare will freeze and remain motionless, hoping to go undetected by its pursuer. At this point the hare is in real danger if the pursuit continues, and is likely to be caught. If open water is nearby, a hare in imminent danger will probably try to swim away from a predator.

On warm summer evenings, snowshoe hares, like rabbits, are frequently seen rolling about on the gravel shoulders of rural roads. These dust baths are taken to loosen shedding fur and to help dislodge fleas and mites. The animals sometimes engage in this behavior in early morning, but most dust baths are taken in the evening because more parasites are contracted while sleeping during the daylight hours.

Eastern Cottontail Rabbit

Immortalized by fables and songs, like "Here Comes Peter Cottontail," this is the most widespread rabbit in North America. Like all rabbits, it differs from hares by having shorter, more rounded ears, a smaller body, and shorter hind legs. Like other rabbits, and unlike hares, the cottontail is a fast short-distance runner that prefers to elude enemies in thick cover, rather than outrunning them across open terrain. Because the cottontail is so common, and because its physical traits, behaviorisms, and diet are generally representative of all rabbits, it has been selected to represent all members of Genus Sylvilagus.

Probably the most adaptable rabbit in the world, the Eastern Cottontail is the most widespread rabbit in North America, and transplanted populations have thrived to the point of becoming pests in Australia and Europe.

Taxonomy:

Kingdom: Animalia
Phylum: Chordata
Class: Mammalia
Order: Lagomorpha
Family: Leporidae
Genus: Sylvilagus
Species: Sylvilagus floridanus

Geographic Range:

Cottontails have the widest distribution of any rabbit in North America. To the north, the species ranges into southern Manitoba and Quebec. Except for Maine, its range covers all of the eastern United States from the Atlantic Coast to North Dakota, and south to Texas, extending through Mexico into Central America and northwestern South America. To the west, cottontail populations are found along the Rocky Mountains from Mexico through eastern Arizona and into Nevada.

Habitat:

Perhaps the most adaptable of lagomorphs, the eastern cottontail is at home in almost any environment that provides drinking water and plenty of cover in which to hide. Historically, the eastern cottontail

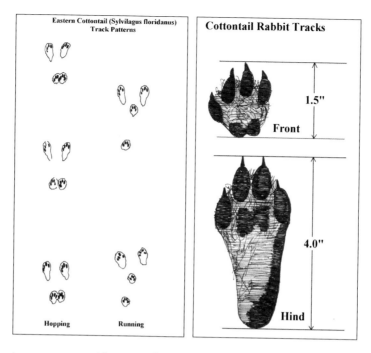

Eastern Cottontail (Sylvilagus floridanus)
Track Patterns

Cottontail Rabbit Tracks

1.5"

Front

4.0"

Hind

Hopping   Running

has inhabited deserts, swamps, coniferous and deciduous forests, and rainforests. Currently, the eastern cottontail seems to prefer "edge environments" between woods and open terrain, including meadows, orchards and farmlands, hedgerows, and clear-cut forests with young trees and brush. The eastern cottontail's range extends into that of six other rabbits, and six species of hares, although, like all rabbits, it prefers less open terrain than hares.

Physical Characteristics:

Mass: Two to more than four pounds.

Body: Typically rabbit-like, with high rounded back, elongated ears two to three inches long, muscular hindquarters, and long hind feet. Head rounded, with short muzzle, flat face, and large dark eyes located at either side. Body length fourteen to eighteen inches.

Tail: Brown on top, fluffy cotton-white below. Length one and one-half to two and one-half inches.

Tracks: Four toes on all four feet. Forefeet nearly round, one to one and one-half inches long. Hind feet elongated, three to four inches long. Claws generally show prominently in tracks. Toes held closely together, not splayed like a snowshoe hare's.

Cottontail scat is largely indiscernible from that of the snowshoe hare, except that the usually spherical pellets are slightly smaller, at just under half an inch.

Scat: Pelletlike, usually spherical or egg-shaped, sometimes flattened discs, usually less than one-half inch in diameter. Color usually dark brown, becoming lighter and more fibrous looking with age. Pellets often deposited in groups of six or more.

Coloration: Brown, grizzled coat interspersed with gray and black hairs, generally uniform over back, sides, top of tail, and head, except for a reddish patch on the nape of the neck. Bottom of tail white and cottonlike. Ears black-tipped. Underside lighter, buff-colored. Cottontails undergo two molts per year: The spring molt occurs from mid-April to mid-July, and leaves a short summer coat that's predominantly brown; from mid-September through October, the brown coat is shed for a longer and warmer grayish winter coat.

Sign: Neatly nipped-off flower and plant stems. Smooth-barked shrubs stripped of bark down to the cambium layer show where rabbits browsed in winter. Oblong "forms" of pressed-down grasses, snow, and sand where a rabbit lay for an extended period while resting or sleeping. Disturbances on graveled road shoulders, made when a rabbit took a dust bath to dislodge parasites and dead fur.

Vocalizations: Normally silent. Vocalizations include a bleating distress call intended to startle a predator into hesitating briefly and giving a surprised rabbit the chance to flee. Bucks (males) chatter and squeal loudly during and immediately after copulation. Nursing does purr while suckling young, and sometimes emit a sharp alarm bark if an intruder approaches too closely to their litters.

Lifespan: Up to five years, but usually less than two years because of heavy predation.

Diet:

The eastern cottontail is believed to be strictly vegetarian, with roughly 50 percent of its summer diet consisting of green grasses, and the balance comprised of wild strawberry plants, clovers, alfalfa, and a broad variety of other ground plants. Its double row of upper incisors allows for chopping tough cellulose fibers into fine clippings that are easier to digest.

Where winter snows make ground plants unavailable, the cottontail diet turns to woody browse, especially the smooth bark of saplings and shrubs, like red osier dogwood, staghorn sumac, rose, lilac, and young poplar, birch, and aspen. Deepening snows actually work for the rabbits by allowing them to reach higher up to get bark and twigs that were previously inaccessible. Cottontails also eat the buds and tender twig ends of most trees, including pines and cedars, and their gnawings have made them a pest to orchard farmers.

Like other rabbits and hares, digestion of tough plant materials is made possible by a process called cecal fermentation, a variation of the cud-chewing process seen in ruminant species. With cecal fermentation, ingested plant material passes completely through the digestive system, where it's partially digested, and is expelled through the anus as green pellets. The predigested pellets are then re-eaten and passed through the digestive tract a second time, where the cellulose is completely broken down and nutrients extracted completely. Cecal fermentation, like cud-chewing, permits rabbits and hares to quickly eat plant foods in places that are inherently dangerous for them to stay, then retire to a more secure location to complete the digestive process.

Usually nocturnal, cottontails may be seen foraging at any time of day in places where they feel safe. In summer, they tend to sleep away the day in cool underground burrows, sometimes in shaded brushy thickets, but increased calorie needs in winter often force them to forage throughout the day. In every season, feeding activities are normally crepuscular, peaking in the first three hours after sunrise, and again in the first two hours after sunset.

Mating Habits:

Like all rabbits and hares, cottontails possess remarkable reproductive powers, which is an indication of their status as food for so many carnivores. Cottontails reach sexual maturity at two to three months of age, and those born during the summer-long mating season are likely to mate before the coming autumn; an estimated 25 percent of the rabbits born in a given summer will be the offspring of juveniles who are less than six months old.

The start of mating season coincides with the spring molt, when adults shed their grayish winter coats for the brown summer coat. The onset of breeding is influenced by lengthening days (photoperiodic), warming temperatures, and the availability of green foods. Bucks, whose testicles are retracted and inert during the winter months, become sexually ready in mid-February, although does aren't normally ready to breed until mid-March. This interval gives adult males a period in which to seek out prospective mates. Both genders remain sexually active until late August or September, with mating season ending earlier for individuals in places where winters come earlier.

Cottontail does are polyestrous, accepting numerous mates, and birthing as many as four litters in a single season. There is no bond between mates, and each go their separate ways after breeding; this promiscuous breeding trait insures a varied gene pool. Prior to mating, cottontails perform a courtship ritual in which the buck chases a doe until she tires, and turns to face him. The pair then rise on hind legs and spar briefly with the forepaws, after which both crouch on all fours, nose to nose, and the male jumps straight upward to a height of about two feet. The female replies by jumping upward, too, and both rabbits may repeat the action several times. The purpose of this jumping behavior is uncertain, but probably demonstrates the fitness of either animal to mate.

Once pregnant, does spurn further advances from males. Gestation lasts an average thirty days, at the end of which expectant mothers retire to a sheltered burrow or hutch, which may be an abandoned marmot den, a natural enclosure under the branches of a fallen tree, even under the floor of an outbuilding. There, in a grass-lined nest that has been insulated with fur nipped from the mother's underbelly and from around her four pairs of nipples, she gives birth to four or five, and sometimes as many as eight, naked and blind (altricial) young. Newborns weigh about one ounce (twenty-five to thirty-five grams), and require constant care. The young grow fast, gaining more than two grams per day, and by five days have opened their eyes.

By two weeks, young cottontails are fully furred and begin to venture outside the nest to feed on vegetation. At this point the mother is nursing them only about twice a day, and may already be pregnant with her next litter. Weaning occurs at about twenty days, and the young rabbits, who may have become intolerant of one another, disperse. Those born in spring or early summer are likely to sire or birth at least one litter before summer's end.

Behaviorisms:

Eastern cottontails are popular with hunters who typically use dogs to chase them into shotgun range, and rabbit meat is very palatable. Not a long-distance runner, an adult cottontail can exceed eighteen miles per hour through thick brush, leaping twelve feet or more, and instantly changing direction by as much as ninety degrees. A flaw in their escape habits, which are effective against predators, is that rabbits run in a circle when pursued, coming back to cross their own trails and thereby confusing the nose of a coyote or bobcat. Human hunters have learned to exploit this by using dogs to chase rabbits back to where they stand.

Cottontails can be taken with a rifle, too. A lone hunter on foot who jumps a rabbit from cover should immediately stop moving, and try to watch where the animal runs to. Being a short-distance sprinter with poor long-distance vision, a cottontail will often duck under a nearby bush and freeze until it is sure there is no pursuit. Many a cottontail has fallen to .22 rifles in this manner.

Cottontails are also a staple of the fur trade. The thin-skinned pelt is silky and thick, and tanned plews are often sold in backcountry gift shops. Other uses include the trim around boot tops, parka hoods, and mittens, and sometimes as an entire fur coat. Rabbit fur isn't water repellent or as long-lived as beaver, ermine, or mink, but it is plentiful, inexpensive, and nice to the touch, and a market exists for plews (prime skins).

Cottontails are not well liked by farmers, gardeners, or landscapers. Their summer feeding and reproductive capacity can mean tremendous damage to crops, while winter browsing of shrubs and fruit trees makes them a pest to golf courses and orchards. The problem is exacerbated by a widespread human reluctance to permit the cottontail's natural enemies to live near homes.

Except for brief encounters during the summer mating season, eastern cottontails are solitary animals that tend to be intolerant of one another. Territorial sizes are dependent on food and other resources, but generally encompass between five and eight acres. Male territories tend to overlap or include the territories of local does.

Every predator large enough to kill a rabbit considers the cottontail prey. Hawks, owls, and eagles hunt them from the air, skunks and other weasels prey on the young, bobcats pounce on them, and coyotes chase them through the underbrush. The rabbits' best defense is to sprint out of sight, then freeze, relying on a maze of trails and scents that can confuse the keenest nose. Most cottontails won't survive into their third year, but reproductive rates are high enough to insure that this species is unlikely to be threatened by hunting or predation.